What they're saying...

"This is a practical guide to overcoming self-sabotage. Pat gives a clear description of the relationship between a positive self image and success."
Harville Hendrix, Best-Selling Author of Getting the Love You Want

"Learning to understand your deserve level is the most significant achievement you will ever make to guarantee your success. Apply the new techniques in this book to guarantee a successful, exciting life."
Peter H. Thomas, Founder of Century 21 Canada, Chairman of the advisory committee of the Young Entrepreneurs Organization

"Your life is not a dress rehearsal. Here is your opportunity to learn to get out of your own way."
Peter McGugan, Psychologist/Best-Selling Author of Beating Burnout: The Survival Guide for the '90s, and When Something Changes Everything

"As an Independent Sales Manager with Weekenders, the success of my business is highly dependent on the success of women I train and sponsor...When I use Pat's techniques, we have extraordinary results."
Susie Nelson, Weekenders

What they're saying...

"Overcoming self-sabotage is vital for peak performance. This book can help you achieve that kind of performance."
James S. Logan, M.D., M.S., former Chief of Medical Operations, N.A.S.A. Johnson Space Center

"God bless you for helping people change their lives for the better."
Mary Kay Ash, Mary Kay Cosmetics

"Pat helped me redefine my life with a new vision. By increasing my 'Deserve Level,' I was able to increase my sales to over $1 million..."
Nestor Vicknair, Merrill Lynch

"One of the ingredients in the growth of my Mary Kay organization from five Directors in 1991 to 35 Directors in 1998 has been Pat Pearson's 'Deserve Level' theory and the practical advice she gives for stopping self-sabotage."
Alia Head, Mary Kay Cosmetics

"I always felt that I deserved the best...but I didn't know what kept me from getting it. Now, I'm starting a new career and my own business...I've upped my Deserve Levels and gotten out of my own way!"
Muriel Funches

STOP SELF-SABOTAGE!

PAT PEARSON, M.S.S.W.

Published by Connemara Press
37 Monterey Pine Drive
Newport Coast, CA 92657

Pearson, Patricia 1950-
Stop Self-Sabotage!
ISBN 0-9665350-0-6

1.Psychology   2. Business   3. Success   4. Self Help

Inquiries should be addressed to:

**PAT PEARSON, M.S.S.W. c/o
PEARSON PRESENTATIONS
37 MONTEREY PINE DRIVE
NEWPORT COAST, CA. 92657**
www.patpearson.com

TABLE OF CONTENTS

~~~

PROLOGUE

~

THE FINE ART OF SABOTAGE

Self-sabotage: We all do it. Old or young. Rich or poor. Famous or unknown. All of our talent, intellect, knowledge and experience cannot help us, for the enemy — the conspirator that whispers in our ear and keeps us from our dreams — is ourselves. But there is hope. When we face our own fears and practice the techniques of change, we can stop sabotaging all our hopes and dreams.

⌘⌘⌘⌘⌘⌘⌘⌘⌘⌘⌘⌘⌘⌘⌘⌘⌘⌘⌘⌘⌘⌘⌘⌘⌘⌘

This book is about what we deserve in life and how we can stop the self-defeating sabotages that keep us from having it.

⌘⌘⌘⌘⌘⌘⌘⌘⌘⌘⌘⌘⌘⌘⌘⌘⌘⌘⌘⌘⌘⌘⌘⌘⌘⌘

"I just don't understand why I can't find a good relationship. They all start out terrific and then... No one wants to make a commitment. Is it bad luck, or is it me? What am I doing wrong?

"I'm in direct sales. I've made $35,000 for the last three years. I feel stuck. Why can't I break through to make $40,000 and more?"

"I'm constantly on diets. I go up. I go down. But nothing ever seems to truly work!"

"I work all the time at my home business, but can't seem to get anywhere financially."

All of these people I have talked with have one thing in common: they're sabotaging their own goals. They don't even realize it — none of us do, because sabotages are unconscious.

If you could change one thing about your life, what would it be? Why don't you think you have it? Many people tell themselves it's bad luck, it's the economy, their mother, or that diets don't work. The truth is, each of the people I just mentioned — and everyone of us as well — practices self-sabotage.

None of us wants second best. Our sabotages cause us to do things that get in our own way. But the good news is you can identify and correct those things. And, it's easier than you ever thought.

If you see yourself in any of these people...Or if there's some important goals you haven't yet reached...**You are sabotaging**.

The fascinating aspect is that we often recognize sabotage in our friends and loved ones, but have a hard time seeing it in ourselves. The fact is, sabotage is what we worry about the most in our children, friends or mates. Will they make their careers work? Will they stop choosing the wrong relationships? Will they take better care of their health? These painful issues concern us all. Throughout our lives we've heard the message, "You can't have it all." If we really have — or become — everything we want we will lose something important. Well, it's time to stop the old tapes and listen to something new. In this book are the stories of men and women who faced their limiting beliefs and moved over, under, around or through their own self-imposed barriers to having the kind of life they wanted. I hope you'll find their stories not only inspirational, but motivational, and that you'll be sharing the story of your own triumph over self-sabotage very soon.

Pat Pearson

~~~

STOP
SELF-SABOTAGE

✻✻✻✻✻✻✻✻✻✻✻✻✻✻✻✻✻✻✻✻✻✻✻✻

PART ONE: IDENTIFYING
SELF-SABOTAGE

✻✻✻✻✻✻✻✻✻✻✻✻✻✻✻✻✻✻✻✻✻✻✻✻

CHAPTER ONE

~

SELF-SABOTAGE AND
THE DESERVE LEVEL THEORY

> *"If I had the mental constitution*
> *to live inside the nutshell and think myself*
> *King of Infinite Space, that would be just fine.*
> *But that's not how I am.*
>
> *"Every man born has to carry his life*
> *to a certain depth or else."*
> **Saul Bellow, <u>Henderson the Rain King</u>**

DESERVE LEVEL — WHAT IS IT?

Your "Deserve Level" is comprised of your conscious and unconscious beliefs about what you can and are supposed to achieve in your life.

I am using the word "level" in its metaphoric rather than literal sense. Just as your Intelligence Quotient is an indicator of your level of intelligence, your Deserve Level Quotient is a gauge of the degree to which you believe you deserve what you want in various areas of life. These Deserve Levels are self-chosen and can be changed.

Of course, you consciously believe you deserve to feel happy, financially secure, loved, free of inappropriate guilt and negativity.

Perhaps you even listen to positive thinking tapes, or tell yourself daily that every day in every way you are getting better and better. And you believe it — consciously.

You were probably taught the myth that if you were kind, obeyed orders and used your head, you would get what you wanted out of life; a sort of award because you had earned it with your good behavior. Conversely, if bad things happened it was probably your fault — "you should have thought about that before you did it" — and you deserved what you got.

This concept of earning or controlling all the outcomes of our lives is flawed. You cannot control major acts of God, the economy, or other people's feelings. That's the bad news.

The good news is, you are in charge of your own choices, feelings and behaviors. That is where you can make a change.

As a psychotherapist I work all day long with people who want more in their lives. I noticed that some people never seemed to get what they wanted. It was too easy for me to shrug it off and say, "Well, they didn't commit to therapy, didn't really work for it." Some of them worked really hard! But they still were not able to achieve what they wanted in their lives.

I began to ask myself, "Why?" With all their genuine motivation and application of techniques, why didn't they improve?

The answer, I believe, is that <u>they didn't believe they deserved to get what they said they wanted</u>. There was an invisible shield between their wants and their ability to create their wants. Every day they ran full speed into this shield, fell over, picked themselves up then did it all over again! This repetition was the most frustrating event of their lives.

I became very much aware of this in my own life.

I grew up in a small Midwestern town in the standard 1950s and '60s way. My father was a successful national book salesman. My mother was a college professor.

I first experienced my own Deserve Level issues after college. Near the end of my senior year I had fallen in love with my college professor. He was young, brilliant, everything I believed I wanted in a romantic partner. I felt swept off my feet.

After graduation, he suggested that I move to Boston to be with him when he started his new job at Harvard. I instantly said "yes." But before we went to Boston, he asked me to travel with his family to Europe for the summer.

I felt I had won an emotional sweepstakes. Cinderella had nothing on me! I joyfully went to Europe and Boston, ignoring my friends' and family's cautions about the man and the move. I was living in Boston, a new city for me, with no job, no friends, and a newly printed degree in Political Science. No one in Boston was particularly impressed with my undergraduate degree, so I ended up selling clothes in Harvard Square.

One night I discovered him with another woman. I was shattered. It was one of those times when the world stops, when one single experience is forever stamped in our memory and changes our entire perception of the world. I had believed we would be married and live happily ever after in Cambridge. I was wrong. My fairy tale dissolved.

After many accusations and tears, I called my parents. They sent me the money to move back home.

I went back in despair. For several weeks I sat, literally sat. I was in terrible emotional pain. I lost weight, felt nauseated, couldn't sleep — or if I did fall asleep, I had nightmares. I had no interest in friends or family.

I was deeply depressed. I walked around with my shoulders pulled almost to my ears. My neck and back were in constant spasms from muscular tension.

My family became very concerned. Here was their daughter, whom they had raised and spent thousands educating, becoming a vegetable in her room. They took me to internists, family friends, clergymen, anyone they could think of to help snap me back to normal functioning. I wouldn't be helped.

Finally they began talking surgery because my shoulders seemed frozen and would not come down. Something in me finally snapped. I said, "Wait a minute. I think every bit of this is emotional."

I remembered a man I had met through friends at college, a psychotherapist. I called him, we talked on the phone, and that phone call, which became my first therapy session, changed my life.

During the call I started to cry and talk about the dream I had lost. After the call, my shoulders came down about half an inch.

I called again the next night. This time I got angry and talked about betrayal and rage. My shoulders dropped another half an inch.

By the end of the week the tension and pain were gone from my shoulders, neck and back. I felt saved. I knew that what happened to me in Boston was something I never wanted to happen again.

I decided the only way I could make sure it didn't happen was to learn everything I could about me and my choice of men. I returned to Dallas and entered therapy with the man who had helped me on the phone.

That is how I discovered that I had a wonderful ability to choose witty, charming men who would never make a commitment to get married. My goal became how to make them change. I fell in love with "potential" and ignored the reality that they did not want the same outcome that I did.

The more they resisted my trying to change them, the harder I tried. None of those relationships were ever changed by my attempts at psychic urban renewal. I wanted to keep the outside while gutting the inside and making them into what I wanted. I failed.

In time I came to understand that at a very fundamental level I did not think I deserved what I had been seeking.

Before you can have more in your life, you have to follow the wise maxim "Know thyself." Not just your Conscious Self, but also your Unconscious Self.

That means changing at a deep and profound level. Some of that change will come quickly and easily. Other parts of it will take longer and will not be easy. It requires a commitment to the evolutionary process that is change.

The rewards can be summed up in one sentence: You can have more in your life than you have ever had.

You are the only person who is entitled to decide what that more will be. Perhaps it is more income, more loving relationships, more sense of safety, more spiritual development, more health and energy.

You already know about the stress and pain of deeply wanting someone or something, yet feeling chronically blocked from getting it. There is such frustration in trying. The painful irony is that trying doesn't work anyway. You may know someone right now who is <u>trying</u> to quit drinking, lose weight, give up a destructive relationship.

The only way not to feel that anguish of frustration is to fully understand and resolve the "how" and the "why" of sabotaging behaviors.

Your final decision on what you deserve is influenced by all your beliefs and feelings, conscious and unconscious. There are specific Deserve Levels for every area of your life: love, work, friends, health. Paradoxically, it is possible to have a high Deserve Level in one area (career) and a low one in another (relationships).

You were born with the fundamental right to believe the best of yourself. This entitlement is basic to every human being. Somewhere along the way, though, we begin to doubt what we deserve.

Babies have no question about their right to be loved or held. They scream when they are hungry or wet, letting the world know of their basic needs. They feel no need to apologize or justify — they just feel it! They ask for what they want and they respond spontaneously when they don't get it.

And then something happens. It is subtle and it takes a long time, but it happens. Our innate sense of deserving to feel our feelings and express our needs starts getting lost as we mature. Instead of believing we deserve love just for "being," we lower our self-esteem and try to earn approval and love by "doing." We begin to think we must earn love, and so we give up our real feelings to meet the approved image.

A two-year-old confidently attempts almost anything. He may not make it, but he will darn well try if he isn't prevented. As we get older, we begin to limit our beliefs about our abilities. We believe the other guy can make the higher grades, get the big sale or promotion, go after the advanced degree, win the beloved. But not us.

These feelings and beliefs sabotage our confidence. They drain our psychic and physical energy. They are like a low-grade infection that is too subtle to diagnose, and the outcome is that we feel defeated before we begin. We may be willing to give it that old college try, but in our hearts we know we are just trying, not succeeding.

Change takes time. Deserving more means you will expand your beliefs, your feelings and your spirituality — expand the limits of your Deserve Level. It is an inner journey, a unification, that becomes an outer reality.

This is not magic. It is a purposeful alignment of your beliefs, choices, focus and energy.

With my clients, as in my own life, I have come to learn that we don't allow ourselves to have what we want until we believe — truly believe — that we deserve it.

Specific wants differ from person to person. One wants to find a husband, another to build a fortune, another to be free from anxiety, another to make a marriage work. Regardless of the wish, there is a vast chasm between what we say we want and what we believe we deserve.

We get what we believe we deserve. No more, no less. ***We never exceed our own expectations, at least not for long.***

Our psychological comfort zones mediate our Deserve Level limits. If we achieve beyond our comfort zone, we face a choice — to increase our Deserve Level limits to encompass this increase, or to give away what we have achieved.

Just as each of us has what has been identified as a "metabolic set point" that controls our bodies, we each have in certain areas of our lives a "psychological set point" that determines our Deserve Level. And as the metabolic set point is operating on an unseen and unconscious level, our psychological set point also operates underground. One has a profound effect on our bodies, the other has a profound effect on our minds — and our behavior. The good news is, that as the metabolic set point can be altered by diet and exercise, the psychological set point can be altered by awareness and a willingness to change. Both can be raised to new levels by identifying and changing the input that created them.

Our beliefs about what we deserve subtly create our reality. We live out the reality of our constraints rather than soaring with the vision of the possible.

To have a full, happy life, we have to be congruent between what we want and what we believe we deserve. The bridge between what we want and what we deserve is our personal expectations.

ⵖⵖⵖⵖⵖⵖⵖⵖⵖⵖⵖⵖⵖⵖⵖⵖⵖⵖⵖⵖⵖⵖⵖⵖⵖⵖⵖⵖⵖⵖⵖⵖⵖⵖⵖⵖⵖⵖ

NEGATIVE EXPECTATIONS = I don't deserve it
(I'll sabotage getting it)

POSITIVE EXPECTATIONS = I deserve it
(I'll facilitate getting it)

ⵖⵖⵖⵖⵖⵖⵖⵖⵖⵖⵖⵖⵖⵖⵖⵖⵖⵖⵖⵖⵖⵖⵖⵖⵖⵖⵖⵖⵖⵖⵖⵖⵖⵖⵖⵖⵖⵖ

Listen to yourself talk about dreams or desires. Do you say "I deserve to have it," or do you say other negative statements?

Before I increased my Deserve Level in relationships, I had a low-level dread and expectation that they would not work out. I <u>wanted</u> to find the man of my dreams but I <u>expected</u> that the relationship wouldn't last. This expectation was based on my lack of self-esteem, my belief system and my personal history.

We cannot always be aware of our unconscious beliefs, but we can see the evidence of them by what we have in our lives. If we can change our Deserve Level, we can begin to expect to get what we want — then we can become congruent with wanting and deserving.

This congruency can lead us to actualizing our dreams.

CHAPTER TWO

~

TALES FROM THE FRONT: STORIES OF SELF-SABOTAGE

"Argue for your limitations, and sure enough,
they're yours."
Richard Bach, <u>Illusions</u>

Self-sabotage psychology can be clearly observed in the personal stories of people who are unaware of how they do themselves in. These stories all contain an unconscious sabotage strategy that wrecks their hopes for a full life.

THE ROOTS OF FAILURE

Susan had a rare gift for connecting with people. After selling hard just to get the job, she made $60,000 her first year in radio sales. She had arrived.

Her "arrival" made her very nervous. Maybe other people at the station wouldn't like the successful Susan. That is what had happened to her in school — it seemed that every time she got an award, the other kids pulled away from her.

The second year she made $40,000.

She says, "I'd like to make more, but I feel uncomfortable being that successful."

Susan grew up poor. The idea that she could make over $20,000 a year was hard for her to believe. Her family was initially proud of her success, but soon began to make veiled disparaging comments about her getting fancier than the rest of them.

She had success, but she **THREW IT AWAY** (her personal sabatoge strategy). At some level Susan believed she didn't deserve it or that she might have to pay for it. She also felt a vague disloyalty to her roots.

LIVING OUT THE PETER PRINCIPAL

Bill was a great insurance salesman. He earned more commissions than anyone in his agency.

His dream was to have his own company. He loved the idea of the challenge and fun of running his own business. When his agency head decided to retire, Bill bought the agency.

Eight months later, Bill could be found staring blankly out the window, yelling at his salespeople, and generally ruining everyone's day. The daily management of an office was killing him.

He was a stellar salesperson, but he was not a manager. He loved interacting with people, hated planning and detail. When his paperwork began to backlog he became rigid, compulsive and irritable.

The sales force, uneasy without effective management, was in mutiny. Bill kept denying the reality of reduced premium flow and declining profits, hoping his "luck" would change.

Bill lost $250,000 before admitting he was in the wrong part of the business. He still could have implemented changes that would have saved his business, but his sabotage strategy of **DENIAL** prevented him from acknowledging reality. What he would not see, he could not change.

THE PERFECT PAIN-IN-THE-NECK

Brilliant, talented, a vice-president of a large multi-national company, Carl was a man on the rise. He did his work flawlessly, came up with innovative techniques, turned in a superb performance. Carl was virtually perfect.

The president of his division respected and liked him. With the employees, however, there was an entirely different scenario. Carl drove everybody crazy with his perfectionism. He corrected everyone's slightest imperfections, pointing out ways they could improve everything from their memo-writing to their exercise programs. He constantly interrupted people and debated the smallest points.

Wherever Carl moved, behind him he left a wake of angry people.

Despite his competence, his interpersonal problems created a **FATAL FLAW** for his ambitions.

CREATING HER OWN REALITY

Cynthia is a beautiful, bright attorney with everything going for her. She is a balanced woman with many interests and friends. She divides her time between a successful law practice, volunteer work with abused kids, and many singles groups and activities.

Extroverted and entertaining, she attracts many men and dates often. That's when her sabotage begins.

She gets in a relationship and really wants it to work. For about six months she is passionately involved with a partner. Then, like clockwork, she decides he is going to leave her.

She won't return the man's phone calls, talk with him, or discuss the problem. She simply withdraws all affection and attention. She emotionally freezes, and resigns herself to being alone again.

As Cynthia says, "I don't want to be one of those women who just hang on long after the love is gone." What she wants is a good relationship. What she has is a long list of ex-boyfriends! Her sabotage strategy is **RESIGNATION**.

NOTHING VENTURED...

David is a shy, intelligent CPA with a large accounting firm. He wants to have a good relationship but gets afraid every time he starts to meet a lady.

He says, "I've always been bashful. I just don't know what to say to the girls I meet — so I don't meet them. I stand in the corner at parties and study my feet."

I told David that he was sabotaging his goal of having a good relationship. He decided to take the plunge and actually meet someone at a party he'd been invited to.

The next week he came into my office feeling very self-satisfied. When I asked what had happened, he said he'd gone to the party and met someone. "I walked into this party and decided I would look over all the women there and select the one I most wanted to meet. I picked her out and then I avoided her at all costs! Later, I met someone else."

David was making some advances, but he was still **SETTLING** for second best.

Susan, Bill, Carl, Cynthia and David are all bright, competent people who managed to find a way to sabotage an achievement they held dear. Their **unconscious sabotage strategies** prevented them from reaching or holding onto their desired outcome.

As one man ruefully said:

> *I always figure out a way to snatch defeat from the jaws of victory!*

He is not alone. Every day of the week intelligent, motivated people do themselves in with *Self-Sabotage*, using strategies of which they may be completely oblivious at a conscious level. Even the current rich and famous have struggled with their own self-sabotage strategies. Tony Robbins talks about his in his book Unlimited Power. Tony came from a background of lack in education, income and knowledge. He literally taught himself to be successful by reading all he could get his hands on. He studied "how" people became truly successful.

At 19, he was named "Wonder Boy" for his phenomenal business success. He had made it, until self-sabotage struck. All this immediate success made him anxious. He felt unworthy and not deserving of all the acclaim. Slowly he began his decline. He gained 38 pounds, and his thriving company was neglected until it was only a shell. As he has said, he woke up every morning thinking obsessively about what he would eat! He nearly torpedoed his entire achievement. Then when he was close to despair, he needed to refocus.

He decided through all his reviews of people and their stories, that education wasn't the answer to being successful. Many educated and knowledgeable people were still struggling. He decided the true road to success was action. That became the basis for his books and tapes on "Personal Power," and that decision has made <u>and kept</u> him a multi-millionaire today.

What sabotage strategies do you use to keep yourself frustrated? The next chapter examines those subtle ways in which we figuratively drive with both the accelerator down and the brake on.

CHAPTER THREE
~
WHAT BEGINS IN FEAR
WILL END IN DEFEAT

> *"We have met the enemy and the enemy is us."*
> **Walt Kelly, Pogo**

Over and over again we see in the media, in our friends and in ourselves how we human beings sabotage ourselves. Sabotages are the single most frustrating part of everyone's life. There is tantalizing anguish in "I just can't get there."

Sabotages are straitjackets on our behavior and our feelings, restraining us from getting what we want, even though we desperately and determinedly want it.

That seems a little perverse — why in the world would we do that? The answer is, we don't do it intentionally; it is unconscious.

We all sabotage; the question is, to what extent do we hurt ourselves? We can sabotage on large levels and on small levels.

Fear is the operative agent in sabotage.

Whatever we fear, if we fear it long enough we will make it happen.

If we fear abandonment, we will abandon first — and often we abandon ourselves as well as someone else.

If we fear rejection, we reject ourselves first. If we fear success, we make sure we don't get it. Failure is bad enough, but success might be worse.

If we fear intimacy, we pick people we can never get close to.

Whatever we fear, if we do not confront and resolve it, the fear wins.

As Gerald Jampolsky says in his book, <u>Love is Letting Go of Fear</u>, "The world we see that seems so insane may be the result of a belief system that isn't working. The belief system holds that the fearful past will extend into a fearful future, making the past and the future one. It is our memory of fear and pain that makes us feel so vulnerable. It is this feeling of vulnerability that makes us want to control and predict the future at all costs."

The paradoxical nature of fear is that by focusing on what we fear, we raise the chances of it happening. By trying to control our lives so it won't happen, we give energy to its occurrence as a sabotage to our dreams.

While raiding his refrigerator for a midnight snack, John Waldrup was suddenly accosted by a burglar. After recovering from his initial fright, John exclaimed: "Before you rob me, I'd like you to meet my wife." The burglar looked at him warily, thinking this was a trap, and John said: "She's been anticipating your arrival every night for 35 years, and I'd hate for her to miss you!"

Most of our fears are imaginary. They have large eyes and see what isn't really there. According to David Seabury, 98% of our fears are unreal and are accentuated by distortion and imaginings. The problem is that they can develop into neurotic fears when we take them too seriously. Because energy follows thought, the more we think or obsess about fears, the more we make them real. We are constantly energizing our fears by our worrying and replaying negative tapes. So we create their reality.

As Thoreau said, "men lead lives of quiet desperation." That desperation is constantly being generated by our fears, and then funneled into our self-sabotages.

In Frank Herbert's science fiction classic <u>Dune</u>, there is a wonderful phrase for dispelling fear.

"I must not fear. Fear is the mind-killer. Fear is the little-death that brings total obliteration. I will face my fear. I will permit it to pass over and through me. And when it has gone past, I will turn the inner eye to see its path. Where the fear has gone there will be nothing. Only I will remain."

The challenge for all of us is to face our fear, to be in charge of it rather than letting the fear be in charge of us. Until we face it, it will win every time — and fear remains the fuel for the vehicle that is our Self-Sabotage.

The first step in mastering fear and raising your **Deserve Level** is to understand your Sabotage Strategies, the ways in which you adjust your life to stay within your self-chosen limits.

SABOTAGE STRATEGIES

1 - THROWING IT AWAY. "I get it, and then, because I don't believe I deserve it, I blow it." (Tony Robbins). "I throw away my dreams." (Susan's story in Chapter 2.)

2 - DENIAL. "I won't pay any attention to this problem. It will just go away." "It's not really that important or significant." (Bill's story.)

3 - THE FATAL FLAW. People who use this strategy may elevate themselves by taking all the right steps but have a crucial personality problem — an addiction, excessive drinking, hair-trigger temper, bi-polar personality disorder, perfectionism — that undoes all their best efforts. (Carl's story.)

4 - RESIGNATION. "Deep down I don't believe I deserve it, so I won't even go after it." "I don't like to get my hopes up. Then, if I don't get it, it won't hurt so much." (Cynthia's story.)

5 - SETTLING. "I want it, but I don't believe I'm good enough, so I'll settle for less." "I won't try very hard because I probably won't get it anyway." (David's story.)

What each of these strategies have in common is an underlying sense of **not deserving** the desired goal. The cornerstone of changing your unconscious sabotage strategies is to become explicitly aware of your own internal Deserve Level. Once you understand that these sabotages have been outside your conscious awareness, then and only then do you have a chance to change them.

EXERCISE 1:

If you were to sabotage an important goal in your life, which sabotage strategy(ies) would you use?

_____

_____

Which one of the personal stories do you identify with the most?

_____

_____

_____

What fear bothers you the most?

_____

_____

_____

_____

CHAPTER FOUR

~

BELIEFS: YOU HAVE TO BE CAREFULLY TAUGHT

"I don't believe it," said Luke Skywalker.
"That is why you fail," said Yoda.
— **"The Empire Strikes Back"**

The song from <u>South Pacific</u> sums up how we all get our belief systems. *"You have to be carefully taught to hate and fear, it has to be drummed into your dear little ear. You have to be carefully taught."*

All of us are carefully taught. In growing up you enroll in an eighteen-year course called LIFE BELIEFS. This course covers all areas of your life — religion, career, style, success, who to marry or not to marry, pleasure, friends, health and so on. This course is quite complete. It's taught to us with daily lessons and homework by experienced teachers, usually our parents. The material they teach us has a lived-in feel because it was taught to them as children.

We absorb our beliefs from these people we grew up with — not always the beliefs they said they had, but always the ones they lived. Many times in therapy I hear clients say, "I sound just like my mother!" They are surprised to realize they are responding in a similar way to their parents' responses. It's shocking but true.

Beliefs are the repetitive statements you make to, and often about, yourself as if they were fact.

Like all of us, you grew up in a family that instructed you in word and deed in what life was to be for you. You were schooled in beliefs and expectations for yourself that were created by others.

Whether you knew it or not, you signed an emotional contract that stated what you were entitled to — but you never saw the small print. It covered your thoughts, decisions, feelings and values.

As you grew up, the power of this emotional covenant continued to assert itself. Your beliefs were reflected in the people you chose to love and be close to, the career you chose to establish, the amount of money you earned, and your level of physical and emotional health.

READING THE FINE PRINT

Some of your beliefs are positive and some aren't. Maybe you were the person in your family who was supposed to be the success, or maybe you were supposed to try hard and barely make it.

Maybe you were programmed to have a wonderful, loving marriage, but can't ever get it together to have a career. Or maybe you were supposed to make it great in a career, but had no skills or example for making a relationship work.

Just because you have permission in one area doesn't mean you have it in another. You have separate beliefs in every area of your life — and your beliefs shape your view of the world.

Joan Motley, a physician friend, told me a story that is a charming example of how a belief shapes your world view. Her two-year-old son had met only his mother's female doctor friends. They went to a picnic with all the doctors from the hospital and he became very excited. He ran up to her and said, "Mommy, Mommy! Men are doctors too!" His whole belief system had shifted.

HOW DO BELIEFS EXERCISE SO MUCH POWER IN OUR LIVES?

There are two reasons why your beliefs are so powerful.

<u>1. Energy follows thought</u>. Your energy follows what you think about. If you stay with a set of negative beliefs, your energy will follow that thought — and consequently you will create more and more negative energy.

You've had days when everything you do doesn't work. You grab your briefcase and it falls open, spilling everything. Your car won't start. You've misplaced your calendar. Everything you touch seems doomed to fail, and you can barely make it through the day.

You stagger home, just glad to be off the highways, and then you get a call from your best friend. He or she has had something wonderful happen and wants to buy you dinner and celebrate — and suddenly you are charged with new energy.

What happened? You were dead, then your thoughts changed and your energy responded.

2. Whatever you think about expands. What you focus on is what you get more of. If you focus on how angry you are at a friend, you are going to find yourself acting madder and madder.

Because your thoughts direct your energy, and the energy you put into your activities then creates outcomes, you have a perfect system of the self-fulfilling prophecy. You get back what you believe will happen even if you consciously want it NOT to happen.

This is the basis for the concept of worry. You worry about money and everything seems to drain your resources. You worry about your health and every ache seems terminal.

On the other hand, you can be excited about a new career or relationship, and you fantasize all the positives. This belief expands and you feel wonderful.

Because of the power of your beliefs, both conscious and unconscious, to dictate your experience, you keep creating what you believe to be true. Consequently, you never exceed your own expectations.

Beliefs are icebergs. Like an iceberg, what sticks up into conscious awareness comprises only about 10 percent of your total belief system. A full 90 percent of your beliefs remain unconscious to your walking-around self, until you go looking for them.

***These unknown beliefs create your thoughts
and direct your energy.***

Rob did not consciously believe that all jobs were precarious. Nonetheless, he unconsciously got the idea that his job would go away some day — so he created what he feared, by setting himself up to be fired.

Without realizing it, Rob was reliving an old family tale. His dad had frequently told him about the Depression, and how you might think you have a good job, but it can get pulled out from under you any time. The only thing you could count on was that your company would never appreciate you. Didn't the railroad let him go after twenty years?

As the story got repeated over and over, Rob created a self-fulfilling prophecy. Symbolically he abandoned his jobs before his jobs had a chance to abandon him. Because he focused his thoughts on his fear, he created what he wanted to avoid.

Our beliefs become so ingrained that our behaviors reflect them in repetitive ways.

Jeff was told by his father, "You'd lose your head if it weren't attached." Jeff still can't keep track of anything! He misplaces car keys, walks away without his purchases, and generally behaves like an absent-minded professor.

HOW DO WE GET OUR BELIEFS?

As we grow up we internalize the feelings, actions and bodily responses of the people around us. Our beliefs are a culmination of all the experiences and messages we have received from parents, siblings, church, school, television, movies and all the myriad messages we take in.

Beliefs become engraved on us early in our lives and, if left unchanged, direct our lives from then on. Some of our beliefs obviously come to us directly, and others are from our interpretations of what people meant.

Other people's comments largely program us. What parents or others say to us is staggering in its importance to our self-esteem and self-confidence.

Shad Helmstetter, in his book <u>What to Say When You Talk to Yourself</u>, gives this example of the amount of negative programming most of us have experienced.

"During the first eighteen years of our lives, if we grew up in a fairly average, reasonably positive home, we were told NO, or what we could not do, more than 148,000 times. If you were a little more fortunate you may have been told NO only 100,000 times, or 50,000 times — however many, it was considerably more negative programming than any of us needs."

Helmstetter goes on to say that behavioral research tells us that as much as 77% of what we think on a daily basis is negative and works against us.

Think about that: <u>whatever good outcomes you are creating are coming from only 23% of your potential positive energy.</u>

Imagine what you can accomplish when you tap into some of that wonderful unused energy!

All day long you listen to this litany in your head that you aren't consciously aware of — but you can feel its drain on your energy system. Many of our most powerful beliefs remain unconscious. They serve as the subtle "glasses," the prescription through which we view the world. Their influence on our lives is profound and our conscious awareness of them is minimal.

Deserve Level starts here and replicates itself over and over through life experience. Deserve Level at this stage has to do with feeling a basic <u>right</u> to get what you want or need.

This belief of one's basic right forms in the earliest object relationship, with mother. If we had "good enough" mothering, we felt nurtured during this crucial early period. When we were hungry, wet, or needed attention — or reached out for closeness or warmth, the "mothering" person was there, responding appropriately.

If a disturbance arose at this time, such as mother becoming ill, depressed, or over-worked, we might have felt deprived. This deprivation becomes interpreted into a belief — a belief that says, "I don't

<u>deserve</u> love, warmth, closeness, because I don't get it when I ask for it."

Small children cannot reason with much complexity, but you can see their beliefs in their behavior. A child whose needs are seldom met becomes increasingly quieter, until at some point he will stop trying. Why keep on asking if no one responds? What's the use?

The baby gives up, feels defeated, and resents the deprivation. Dr. T. Berry Braselton, the noted pediatrician and child behaviorist, says he can tell by the time a child is nine months old whether she has decided she will or won't make it in the world.

One basic limiting belief states: "If I have to ask for it, it is not worth getting." Kyle will not ask for what he wants, unconsciously battling between the part of him that hopes Heather will "notice" and his belief that she never will. His corollary belief, of course, is "If she loved me, she would know. If I have to ask her, it means she doesn't care."

It is an unintentional set-up to Heather, a no-win situation for everybody. She goes crazy trying to guess what he wants.

It gets even deeper. The second part of Kyle's belief is, "If she responds after I ask her, it's only because of obligation and guilt, and I don't want her to give me anything for those reasons." Or maybe the noble version, "I don't want to impose on her if she doesn't want to do it."

A set-up? Of course. Intentional? No. Kyle's belief system can only acknowledge Heather as caring when she happens to guess right about what he wants. His belief about himself — his sense of what he deserves — is very low.

Art Linkletter told a story about a little boy who exemplified a very positive belief system. For several years Art hosted a television program called the "House Party." He invited small children to be on his show. He enjoyed their candor. He always asked, "Tell me what your mother told you not to say" — and they did!

One day he had on a very precocious child named Scott and asked him, "How were you selected to be on my show?" Scott replied, "I'm the smartest kid in my class." Art said, "That's very good. Did your teacher tell you that?" Scott said, "No, I noticed it myself!" Now that's a positive belief system.

Let's get back to you and your beliefs.

EXERCISE:

Think of one thing you want, and write it down. It can be anything — a relationship, career, more money, more and better friends, more spiritual development. Focus on just this one thing for the moment.

Successful Pampered Chef career —

Big Sales; big downline

WHAT I WANT:

Now write down your positive and negative beliefs about this thing you want. For example, you may want a powerful and successful career. The positive belief would be, "I'll have freedom and money to do what I want." The negative might be, "If I'm successful, I can't also have a happy marriage."

POSITIVE BELIEFS ABOUT GETTING WHAT I WANT:

1. _I will have financial success_
2. _I will work for myself; control my_
3. _I will help others_ _work_

NEGATIVE BELIEFS ABOUT GETTING WHAT I WANT:

1. _I may not be able to build it big_
2. _____
3. _____

Remember: The negative beliefs you have about what you want are a predominate issue in your self-sabotage.

As you will see, they play an important part in your Self-Esteem and Self-Confidence.

CHAPTER FIVE

~

DEFINING SELF-ESTEEM AND SELF-CONFIDENCE

"To be nobody but yourself in a world that tries its best day and night to make you everyone else, is to fight the hardest battle anyone can fight and never stop fighting."
John Pearson

Self-esteem and self-confidence are often thought of as emotionally the same. Many of us use the words interchangeably. I believe they are very different.

To have a real sense of **SELF ESTEEM,** you have to believe that you're lovable. I knew from my mother that she'd love me even if I burned the house down. She had a distinct preference that I didn't do that and I never did, but I knew she'd still love me. Her loving was unconditional. She loved me for my "being," my personhood. I could, and did, spend hours in my room listening to my records and eating Twinkies, being very unproductive, and she'd still love me. In unconditional loving there are no "have to's" or demands to do something to be loved. It isn't earned, it is given.

Our level of **SELF CONFIDENCE** is based on the knowledge that we can <u>do</u> something worthwhile in life. When I was younger I would get out my red wagon and sell my comic books and lemonade. My dad, who was a national sales manager for a large book company, would walk by and say, "That's my girl. You're a chip off the old block." I'd get a great deal of praise for producing. The same was true when I brought home A's on my report card. I learned that I could do some things and my self-confidence slowly grew.

I knew my mother loved me no matter what I did or didn't do. She also wanted me to excel and do well, so I felt her support in both areas and was clear that they were separate in her mind. She loved me (self-esteem) and believed in my abilities to achieve (self-confidence).

With my Dad I wasn't so sure. I knew that he'd approve of me if I got good grades or performed well (self-confidence), but I wasn't so sure that he'd love me if I didn't produce. (The truth is, he loved me all the time. I just didn't believe it until later in life.)

This developed into my adult **Deserve Level.** I felt loved and supported by women for myself and my achievements, but believed I had to perform for men to "earn" their love. I felt I had to "dance for Daddy" or he wouldn't love me. Of course, that never worked because you can't "earn" love. It has to be given freely.

For a number of years, until I learned that, I tried hard to earn men's love and drove them away in the process. I kept producing and doing things to get them to love me. If a man in my life needed something, I took on the burden of making that happen — a new job, more money, whatever. I felt if I did enough to prove my worth and loyalty then surely he would reward me by loving me.

It didn't work that way. After a lot of failed attempts and with the help of some good therapy, I decided to give up dancing for Daddy's and men's approval. I felt really scared because I believed if I ever stopped working hard for love, I wouldn't get even the meager amount of love I was receiving.

I was so scared of not doing it right that my tension level was very high. I would wake up sometimes with my heart racing and feeling a little nauseated, all because I wasn't sure the man in my life really loved me. This anxiety was overwhelming. I would try and channel my anxiety into "productive" activity, for example, doing what I thought would make him love me. I would go shopping for myself and end up buying him ties, sweaters, etc. I would plan to be with my girlfriends and then, if he called, I would cancel. I was puppy-dog eager to be helpful, loving and approved of.

My desperation to be loved was more than apparent. Men, having a built-in radar for desperate women, would quickly move away from me.

Finally, all the disappointment and heartbreak got to be too much. I entered therapy. In that process I started working on building my self-esteem and learned to stop manipulating men to give me my own approval. Only I could do that.

I felt tremendous relief. You mean I don't have to try hard to figure out how to make him love me? You mean that's not the answer to my feelings of loneliness or despair? I began a long process of loving me first, building my self-esteem, and increasing my Deserve Level in relationships.

SELF-ESTEEM AND SELF-CONFIDENCE IN BUSINESS

Mike is an extremely self-confident salesperson in the computer industry. He is convinced that his product is the best and all potential prospects would buy it if they just knew about it. He knows that he is in control of his sales, his income and his professional life. He is always the top producer in his company and his income reflects it.

At the same time, Mike is not happy in his personal life. Try as he will, he has never had a relationship last longer than two years. The truth is that while his self-confidence is high, Mike's self-esteem is shaky. Because he feels unsure of himself in his relationships, he tries to <u>do</u> things to feel better, working harder and harder. The more he works and produces, the more his self-confidence increases. Regrettably, that doesn't change his self-esteem.

Self-confidence is conditional
acknowledgment for your performance.
You are acknowledged for
"<u>doing</u>" something well.

*Self-esteem is unconditional
acknowledgment for your
own worth and lovability. You are
acknowledged for "<u>being</u>" a good person.*

Confusion between self-esteem and self-confidence creates massive stress in our lives. Because we get them intermingled in our perception, we tend to "scratch the wrong itch," to compensate inappropriately.

For healthy self-confidence you either have to do something or have reason to believe, based on past performance, that you can. You have to make your quota, or put together a great deal, or run a five-minute mile.

For healthy self-esteem you need acknowledgment of who you are as a person, that you are loved and lovable just the way you are.

Self-confidence is fostered in a child by encouragement for being capable. The father who gives an "Attaboy" to his kid for sinking the baskets, the mother who teaches him how to ride his bike and praises his efforts, are helping him build his self-confidence. That pride of accomplishment and capability becomes transferable — if he knows how to rewire a lamp cord, he is likely to tackle another rewiring job with a degree of certainty.

Self-esteem comes from being told he is a terrific kid, whether he is doing something or not. It tells him about his worth as a person. It is not conditional upon his performance.

JANE'S STORY

If we are loved, self-esteem can be gained even through great adversity.

In this excerpt from her motivational speech, Jane, a national public speaker, talks about self-esteem and the awesome power of love.

"One rainy August afternoon two little sisters, four and seven, were driving their mother crazy, running and romping through the house. She decided to entertain them. She boiled some eggs, gave one to each child, put them in the living room on a piece of paper, and said, 'Look, I want you to take some crayons, paint a face on your eggs, and make some egg dolls. When you get finished making them, we'll have a play with them and then we'll eat the characters.'

"As the girls were engrossed in their art work, the mother went to answer the doorbell. The four-year-old finished painting her egg in about two minutes, ran to where her mother was standing at the front door visiting with a neighbor, and said, 'I want another egg.' Her mother answered, 'Wait just a minute.'

"The little girl went to the kitchen, pulled a stool up to the stove, crawled up on the stool, and pulled the pot forward to get another egg. As she put her hand in, got burned, and when she jerked back and fell off the stool, she brought the pot down with her.

"Half a gallon of boiling water poured over that little four-year-old body. She was burned from her neck to her knees — about three-quarters of her body. She spent seven months in the hospital, with every complication a burn victim can endure. The worst was that her teeth all rotted and fell out, and every week they came in with the razors and shaved her head. But she lived, and that was a miracle.

"Her parents were so delighted that their daughter had made it through the ordeal, they forgot to tell her what she looked like. When it came time to go home, she was not prepared for what she would find.

"The first thing she was going to do was to go to Sunday School. For this little girl that meant to have fun. It had been a long time since she had had any fun. That Sunday morning she got up very early — she was so excited about finally getting to do something. It was like Christmas morning.

"She went to her Sunday School class, but she didn't have fun. Nobody would have anything to do with her. The children were frightened of her, some of them laughed at her, and nobody played with her. When her mother came to pick her up, she looked down at her child and saw that the burns had healed but that the emotional scars were very deep.

"She took her little girl home and put her up on the bed. And this is what that mother told that child that day.

"She said, **'What is beautiful about you is on the inside.'**

"And that mother told that little girl those words every single day. She never missed one day. Sometimes the child would come in from playing and say, 'Everybody hates me because I am so ugly.' And the mother would say, 'Oh, no, I love you. And you're beautiful. Look inside.'

"When she went to the first grade, she didn't look a lot better. She still didn't have any teeth. Her scars were very prominent and her hair grew in funny patches. There were parents that actually called the school and said, 'My child can't learn if he has to sit next to that burned one.'

"By the time she was eight, she got her teeth, her scars were beginning to fade, the children were used to her, and it seemed that her life was going to be very normal.

"However, when she turned nine she had another major setback. She became a cancer patient.

"She was one of the first children in that little southern town ever to have chemotherapy, and it saved her life. She again lost her hair.

"From the time she was four until she was thirteen, there are no pictures of that child — except for the one that the mother put in the little girl's mind, and that was, **'You are beautiful. Look inside.'**

"I was that child. That was my childhood."

Jane tells this story, not for pity, but for illustration. We all have scars, emotional and physical, and we need a healthy self-esteem to survive those experiences.

ELLEN'S STORY

Ellen Terry is a charming, attractive woman in her mid-forties with two children. Fifteen years ago she was the wife of a very successful banker, living a lifestyle we would all envy. She divided her time between important charities, tennis, Junior League and friends.

One afternoon, while she was hosting a charity tea, there was a knock on the door. She answered and was told by the man on her doorstep, "I've come to repossess your Mercedes."

Ellen first thought there had been a mistake. Her disbelief turned to dismay as she learned that no payments had been made on the car loan in months. Thus began a devastating nightmare that included financial ruin, divorce and a seven-month separation from her two children, who went to live with their grandparents while Ellen tried to figure out what to do.

She began by liquidating all her assets in an effort to pay creditors. Her house, jewelry, most of her clothes, everything had to go. Even then, she was still left owing more than $100,000 to the IRS.

Ellen Terry had no car, no job, no apparent workplace skills. She did, however, have a legacy from childhood — a feeling of self-worth given to her by her parents. She'd been told to be a fighter, not a quitter.

She says, "My dad, who was all of 5-foot-5-inches and wore size 5 cowboy boots, always told me the only inches that mattered were the six inches between your two ears, and whether you perceived things positively or negatively. He taught me that perceiving the glass as half-full or half-empty is up to you." She pulled herself up to her full 4-foot-10-inch height and started fighting.

Her first goal was to get a job quickly, one that would make enough money for her to bring her kids back home. On her brother's advice, she decided to pursue residential real estate. Most people, she says, discouraged her, saying it was not a promising career and would take six months to a year to make a sale. Undaunted, she tenaciously interviewed real estate companies. Finally she persuaded Coldwell Banker, then the largest nationwide real estate company, to give her a chance.

She says, "I felt like the rabbit that was being chased by the fox. When the farmer yelled out, 'Hey rabbit, you gonna make it?' The rabbit hollered back, 'Make it? Man, I gotta make it!'"

The day she passed the exam she wrote her first contract. Within six weeks she had sold two houses and made $12,000. By the end of her first full year she was Coldwell Banker's top salesperson in Texas and second in the nation.

A couple of years later she opened her own company, which is known in Dallas as the "Neiman-Marcus of residential real estate." It has logged over a billion dollars in residential sales, many representing multi-million dollar homes.

Ellen Terry says, "I believe there are absolutely no restrictions on what you can do except the ones you create in your own mind. Success is a matter of being committed to excellence in whatever you do."

HIGH SELF-ESTEEM,
LOW SELF-CONFIDENCE

Look at Margaret, the 50-year-old affluent housewife who has many wonderful, loving relationships. She is at a time in her life when her children are grown, her husband has retired, and she also has retired from her mothering role. She is tired of volunteer work and she wants to do something in the marketplace, to produce. She has high self-esteem but low self-confidence, because she is thinking of entering an area that is new to her. Because she devoted most of her adult life to caring for her family, she does not have the experience to reassure herself that she will be able to perform well in the business world.

"I'd love to go into cosmetic sales," she says, "but I'm just terrified. I don't know if I can do it. What if I fall flat on my face? I want to try, but I'm just too scared."

Her self-esteem is okay. It's her self-confidence that she needs to work on.

HIGH SELF-CONFIDENCE,
LOW SELF-ESTEEM

Ironically, whether we lack self-confidence or self-esteem, we tend to make up the deficiency by using the skills we have in the opposite arena.

Mike, the salesman, for example, used his ability to perform and produce when he tried to create good relationships. He would try to razzle-dazzle and charm his partner, trying to "make her love him." Naturally, this just didn't work. You can't "sell" anyone on loving you. You can only be yourself — and either they do or they don't.

People with high self-confidence and low self-esteem tend to be pretty structured and goal-directed. This is a good work habit, but when you bring it home, you try to control your mate and run the show. These people often have a great deal of interpersonal difficulty; the skills that work well in one area may not in the other.

To compensate, they throw themselves into their job for comfort and they overachieve. Often they make work a substitute for social life or friends.

At work they seem to have it made, but in their personal life they are so out of balance that they try to nurture themselves with destructive outlets like excessive drinking, illegal drugs or compulsive sexual encounters.

On the other hand, the person with high self-esteem but low self-confidence might trade on his people skills to the detriment of performance. Sales managers have heard it often: "I'm a nice person, a good guy, and we're friends. Come on, keep me on board even though I never make my quota."

As a manager, you don't want to fire such people because they really are likable — but the truth is, they just can't produce.

44

Managers are also familiar with the person who is fabulous as a producer but is a nightmare to work with. Joyce is one of those. A top producer in commercial real estate leasing, Joyce simply can't seem to get along with any manager. She sees them all as parental figures, and she rebels. She refuses their direction, talks back, tells them they don't know what they're talking about.

Joyce refuses to let anybody have authority over her.

Joyce also keeps getting fired.

Her sales performance is superb, but she is so horrible to deal with, it's finally just not worth it to the beleaguered manager or, indeed, the organization. Joyce sabotages herself because of her low self-esteem.

There are two important and different aspects operating: likability and productivity. A person who is simply likable but does not produce is bad for the company. A person who is a great producer but is hard to deal with may be good for the company in the short haul, but bad when everyone gets fed up with the prima donna tactics.

Here's a wonderful illustration of a great balance of self-esteem and self-confidence:

THE LITTLE MERMAID

Robert Fulghum, in his delightful book <u>All I Really Need to Know I Learned in Kindergarten</u>, tells about trying to get a wired-up group of grade-schoolers to take part in a game of Giants, Wizards, and Dwarfs.

As the pandemonium reached critical mass, he yelled out to the kids that they had to decide <u>right now</u> which they would be — a GIANT, a WIZARD, or a DWARF. As the groups consulted, Fulghum felt a tug at his pants leg.

A small child stands there looking up, and asks in a small, concerned voice, "Where do the Mermaids stand?"

A long pause. A very long pause. "Where do the Mermaids stand?" says I.

"Yes. You see, I am a Mermaid."

"There are no such things as Mermaids."

"Oh, yes, I am one!"

She did not relate to being a Giant, or a Wizard, or a Dwarf. She knew her category. Mermaid. And was not about to leave the game and go over and stand against the wall where a loser would stand. She intended to participate, wherever Mermaids fit into the scheme of things. Without giving up dignity or identity. She took it for granted that there was a place for Mermaids and that I would know just where.

Well, where DO the Mermaids stand? All the "mermaids" — all those who are different, who do not fit the norm and who do not accept the available boxes and pigeonholes?

Answer that question and you can build a school, a nation, or a world on it.

What was my answer at the moment? Every once in a while I say the right thing. "The Mermaid stands right here by the King of the Sea."

...It is not true that Mermaids do not exist. I know at least one personally. I have held her hand.

~~~

HOW DO YOU STACK UP?

It is critical to balance your self-confidence and self-esteem. Why? Because you are a whole person. Eventually you will pay the price for being out of balance.

If you have more self-confidence than self-esteem, you may be nice and charming, but you tend to get addicted to work and try to get it to take the place of close relationships. You probably don't have a support system.

If you have more self-esteem than self-confidence, you are thoughtful, considerate, and feel good, but you may lack drive. Less achievement-oriented, you get excited by having good relationships, even at work, and you may not want to concentrate on business.

WHERE ARE YOU?

In **Self-Esteem** I rate myself:
1   2   3   4   ⑤   6   7   8   9   10

In **Self-Confidence** I rate myself:
1   2   3   4   5   6   7   ⑧   9   10

Whichever one gets the lower rating is the groove on the record where your needle always gets stuck. It is the one you think about when you're driving home alone after work. If your love life is terrible, you'll focus on that. If your sales are off, you'll focus on that. Whichever it is, you need to do the things that will bring you into balance.

Inside all of us is the need to finish our unfinished business, to bring the two aspects of our lives into balance.

If you lack self-confidence, start paying attention to things you do well. Get acknowledgment from others. DO the things it will take to get that increased self-confidence.

If you lack self-esteem, give yourself time to be with people and share feelings, get to know them, and put aside work-oriented activity as the only way of life. Focus on liking, loving and feeling. Those are the reasons we are alive.

EXERCISE 3:

<u>SELF ESTEEM ASSESSMENT</u>

I'M LIKABLE BECAUSE...

_____

_____

I'M LOVABLE BECAUSE...

_____

_____

I WANT TO GROW IN SELF ESTEEM BY BEING MORE...

_____

_____

SELF CONFIDENCE ASSESSMENT

I WANT TO GROW IN SELF CONFIDENCE BY DOING MORE...

_____

_____

_____

I'M CAPABLE AND ABLE TO DO...

_____

_____

_____

I'M CONFIDENT ABOUT MY...

_____

_____

_____

HIGH SELF-ESTEEM + HIGH SELF-CONFIDENCE = HIGH SELF-WORTH

How you live your life is up to you. If you balance your self-esteem and self-confidence, you will find that they comprise a healthy sense of self-worth. If you do what it takes to bring your life into balance, you will have few regrets, because your business and personal life will bring you the rewards you seek — a high Deserve Level and an enhanced passion for being alive.

CHAPTER SIX

~

YOU NEED PERMISSION FROM YOUR PAST

"The past is prologue."
— Inscription on the
Treasury Building,
Washington, D.C.

All of us grew up in families that gave us or withheld permission for success. Some of us had families that cheered us on at whatever we wanted to achieve. Others came from families that were more cautious, a little scared for us, and their admonitions held us back.

Within this culture there are specific roles that men and women get told they can do. If you wanted to do something that was out of that role, you may not have received permission to do it. Then you had to struggle with giving yourself permission.

Your programs for living — what you heard about yourself, or what your parents did with their lives, the models they showed you — are part of your permission system.

You inherited your permissions from all the stories, myths and statements that your family or important mentors made about you. You were told about your abilities, in word and behavior, by the people closest to you. Your personal beliefs about yourself are scripted into your permissions system. These permissions follow you and direct your life's course.

Maybe you are a "people person," an extrovert just like Dad. Dad happens to be a top-ranked insurance salesman, so naturally you'd be good in sales.

Sometimes your permissions come from important people other than your parents. Jim's leadership abilities were anchored into his unconscious by a strong relationship with his parish priest.

Jim was trained in life lessons by the Jesuits' beliefs in service and sacrifice for others. He became the youth fellowship president of his church club. One afternoon his mentor came up to him, took hold of his arm, and said, "You will be a very important man one day. You are a leader of men."

This permission went right through to Jim's unconscious and became a powerful psychological imprint. He grew up to become a recognized leader in the broadcasting field and a highly active community leader.

Some of us have a **lack of permission** from our past. When we start to go after something, we run into blocks and sabotage ourselves because inside ourselves we don't believe it is possible. This can create enormous conflict within us.

Phyllis wants to have a successful career and also be a loving, effective wife and mother. When she was growing up she saw women who did one or the other, but no one who did both successfully. Her mother never believed that she could have both. Phyllis has to create new permission, based on role models she sees now, women who do manage to balance several roles and still take care of themselves.

Maybe you got **mixed permission**. From one parent you may have heard, "You can't do that!" and from the other "That's great, kid, you can do it!" When you start to move toward a new goal that pushes you beyond your comfort zone, you get two messages in your head. Guess what? Your action becomes ambivalent, one step forward and one step back, depending upon which permission is more active at that moment.

A lot of people got mixed permission from the same parent. One time we'd hear one thing, and another time another. It takes some sorting to figure out what you have been paying most attention to.

Sometimes a parent says one thing and acts another, which means you may have learned to do the same thing. The classic line is, "Do what I say, not what I do."

Your parents did the best job they could and loved you the very best way they knew how. Sometimes what you heard was not what they said, but rather how you interpreted it out of your own perception.

Your parents may now have tremendous support for you without your realizing it. The limitations they placed on you when you were small may have long since disappeared in their minds but not in yours.

A lot of people live out the permission they had at age five, and if they do not update, they will stay the same.

If you believed you were shy, retiring, and could not have good relationships back then, unless you change that early program, you live it out your whole life.

Think about what your family said about relationships. Does everyone in your family stay happily married, or is divorce the accepted way? Is your father or mother the boss or the negative one? What kind of opposite-sex partner are you attracted to? Do they remind you of your parent?

Sally had spent thousands of dollars on therapy and still could not seem to make a relationship work. She did an exercise in my seminar in which she closed her eyes and told her mother what she wanted (which was a fifth husband), then clearly heard her mother say, "Don't fool with them, they'll all leave you anyway." No wonder none of her relationships ever lasted.

The challenge is for you to give yourself **new permission** to let yourself believe you can have what you want. You can find other sources, within yourself and from other people, to get the permission you do not currently have.

Money is another powerful issue in our permission systems. How did your parents handle money? See yourself asking your parents for money... What did they say? How did they feel about people who had or didn't have money? What was money to be used for — fun, savings, or just to squeak by? How much is enough? Did they believe that you could make money?

Sue was making about thirty thousand dollars a year in real estate sales commissions and was frustrated because she could not seem to make more. In discussing her Deserve Level with me, she discovered that her father had never made more than thirty thousand dollars a year — and she believed that if she did better than her father, he would not love her any more. Her mother had died, her marriage had ended, and her dad's love was much more important to her than the additional money.

Every time she started to make more, she got sick, got fired, or found some other way to sabotage herself.

When she began the process of increasing her Deserve Level, she contacted her father in west Texas and asked him pointblank how he felt about the money issue. His reply was, "Why, darlin', you make all the money you can and want to! I'll come to Dallas and let you buy me a steak dinner."

A few months later she got into computer sales. Her first commission was $15,000, half of what she had formerly made in six months. Her annual earnings that year were $150,000! She did so well that she broke every sales record in her company — by getting out of her own way. She found out where her permission stopped, where the conflict was and resolved that conflict. I told her that if I'd had a higher Deserve Level, I'd have charged her a commission, not a flat fee!

How about permission for health? Are you in a "heart attack family?" What are your family's stories about longevity and personal health? At what age do you expect to get ill, or do you expect to stay healthy until you die?

Few people will find it productive to actually go back to their parents and try to get the permission they did not get thirty years ago. You will know by your behavior what you got and did not get. There is no magic in this: just look at your outcomes, at what you are doing, and from them you will be able to trace back to the origins.

Once you know what it is that your internal permission system has not been allowing you to have, you can change it. Until then, you are stuck into blaming outside factors.

We look for excuses, we pass the buck, if we will not take responsibility for how we are blocked:

"The economy is lousy."
"There are no good single men/women left."
"It was office politics."
"They discriminate against people like me."
"I was so good I intimidated them."
"It's all my husband's/wife's fault."

You have the power not only to find out how you are blocked, but also the power to change it. That is a lot better, isn't it, than thinking that life is "doing it" to you — because from that position you do not have any power.

As Wanda Wolfe so profoundly states in her letter:

"When I heard you speak at our Weekenders conference you talked about getting permission from our pasts. This is when I realized what was holding me back. It was Me!

I came from a very poor family that dealt with hardship as the way of life. My father (born in 1886) was a coal miner with a quick right hand for discipline and a third-grade education. He only gave criticism, never love or encouragement. My mother had a seventh-grade education and didn't think anyone needed more than that. I was afraid to be smarter than they were. I heard their voices from my childhood saying "Don't be such a smart-aleck! Keep your big mouth shut!" So I did. I was afraid to ask questions or voice my opinion about anything. My mom's favorite saying when asked for anything we couldn't afford (which was almost everything) was, "Don't ask for things you can't have. That's stupid."

I knew I had to get out of my own way if I was to become successful. So I did as you suggested and got a picture of my parents and starting talking to them honestly for the first time. I certainly couldn't do that when they were alive. It was quite difficult at first, but I continued talking to them. I even forgave them.

You talked about people who were afraid to earn more money than their parents, but got permission to do so. Ah! I knew that I had already earned more than both my parents combined, but didn't want to be a "smart-aleck"—so I was holding myself back. Then I asked for their permission. Guess what? It was given! I'm still doing the self-talk and affirmations after two years. I have raised my self-esteem, have confidence in myself that I <u>never</u> had, and have reached the goal of becoming a sales manager. I deserve it!

Wanda Wolfe
Concord, CA

DIAGNOSTIC EXERCISE:

Think of something you want for yourself. It can be anything — more money, better love life, a new car, anything.

Now fantasize that you're talking with your father and you tell him what you want for yourself. What is his response? How does he look? What is he saying? Is he supportive, disbelieving or critical?

Now pretend you are talking with your mother. What is her response? Look at her face. Is she with you or not? What does she say about your wants?

Review your parents' different responses. Who do you feel supported by? Do you have permission to get what you want?

What are the messages you got from your parents? You may still treat yourself the same way you were treated. If you didn't like any of the responses you got, check to be sure that you are not still giving yourself these same messages.

Give yourself a few minutes to think about all this. Jot down what permissions you do or do not have, and star the ones you want to have more of.

PERMISSIONS FROM MY PAST
(RE: SUCCESS, LOVE, HEALTH)

(1) From Mother
Positive Permissions
Success:_____

_____

Love:_____

_____

Health:_____

_____

Negative Permissions
Success:_____

_____

Love:_____

_____

Health:_____

_____

(2) From Father
Positive Permissions
Success:_____

_____

Love:_____

_____

Health:_____

_____

Negative Permissions
Success:_____

_____

Love:_____

_____

Health:_____

_____

(3) From Significant Other (Wife, Husband, Boyfriend, Girlfriend)
Positive Permissions
Success:_____

_____

Love:_____

_____

Health:_____

_____

Negative Permissions

Success:_____

_____

Love:_____

_____

Health:_____

_____

Now that you understand the unconscious power of **permission from your past,** you are ready to move into a powerful new phase: deciding what you really want. Not what others wanted for you, not what you are "supposed" to want, but what <u>you</u> really want.

CHAPTER SEVEN
~
DISCOVERING WHAT YOU WANT: NAME IT TO CLAIM IT

"We all hear the burning voice, I want."

Saul Bellow, <u>Henderson, The Rain King</u>

As with any journey, before you can map your route you have to know where you are starting.

IDENTIFYING YOUR DESERVE LEVEL
Quickly and spontaneously, circle your answers to these questions:

Next year, I believe I will make the following income (in dollars):

1)	10-15,000	8)	125-150,000
2)	15-30,000	9)	150-200,000
3)	30-45,000	10)	200-250,000
4)	45-60,000	11)	250-300,000
5)	60-75,000	12)	300-400,000
6)	75-100,000	13)	400,000+
7)	100-125,000		

I believe I can have the material things I want.
1) Never
2) Almost never
3) Sometimes
4) Most of the time
5) Always

I believe I can have a good, loving relationship.
1) Never
2) Almost never
3) Sometimes
4) Most of the time
5) Always

I feel lovable and capable of loving others.
1) Never
2) Almost never
3) Sometimes
4) Most of the time
5) Always

I feel I can produce and perform well at my job or career.
1) Never
2) Almost never
3) Sometimes
4) Most of the time
5) Always

I would rate my love life:
1) Very low satisfaction
2) Medium low satisfaction
3) Medium satisfaction
4) Medium high satisfaction
5) High satisfaction

I would rate my work life (income, work climate, liking of my job):
1) Very low satisfaction
2) Medium low satisfaction
3) Medium satisfaction
4) Medium high satisfaction
5) High satisfaction

I would rate my social contacts and friends:
1) Very low satisfaction
2) Medium low satisfaction
3) Medium satisfaction
4) Medium high satisfaction
5) High satisfaction

I feel capable of getting what I desire from life:
1) Never
2) Almost never
3) Sometimes
4) Most of the time
5) Always

My parents (or divide between mother and father for separate ratings) believe I'm a worthwhile, competent and lovable person:

1)   Never
2)   Almost never
3)   Sometimes
4)   Most of the time
5)   Always

SCORING

Add up the numbers of the answers you circled.

Below 20 points - Low Deserve Level

You don't truly believe you can have much in your life. Take a serious look at changing your thoughts and the statements you make to yourself about who you are and what life holds. You may want to get some counseling — your beliefs about yourself are stopping you from prosperity.

21-30 points-Moderate Deserve Level

You believe you deserve some of life's rewards, though you block the full attainment of these good feelings and events. Some directed imagery and more positive visualization of the desired outcomes would certainly move you forward.

32 - 43 points - Higher Deserve Level

You are more consistently in line with your positive beliefs of yourself and the world. Keep up the good work. Any hesitations or dips in self-esteem or self-confidence should be treated immediately to insure continued improvement. You're on the way!

44 or higher-Very High Deserve Level

You are being/doing everything right. You probably are enjoying a great many benefits from your participation in life. No doubt you are a pleasure to know and associate with, both personally and professionally.

~~~

Now you know where you currently are in your overall Deserve Level. The next step to increasing your Deserve Level is to answer this very hard question: "What do I want?"

The next step is to identify where you want to go and what is stopping you from getting there.

THE WANTS TRACKDOWN

This exercise requires that you ask a friend to be your partner, Player A. You are Player B. Later you can reverse roles.

PHASE 1: Awareness

Sit facing each other. Player A looks at Player B and asks: 'WHAT DO YOU WANT?" and B answers whatever comes to mind. A acts as Scribe for B and writes down the answer, then A again asks, "WHAT DO YOU WANT?" and B gives another answer. Write it down, and again: "WHAT DO YOU WANT?"

Do not get sidetracked with comments, agreements, or chat — just repeat the exercise over and over for at least five minutes.

WHAT DO YOU WANT?

_____

_____

_____

_____

When you have responded many times, you may be surprised by some of your answers. You may reach a level of wanting that you have not been aware of.

PHASE 2: Sabotage Strategies

Same procedure as before, but this time the repeated question is, "HOW ARE YOU SABOTAGING GETTING WHAT YOU WANT?" Answer this question for every want you listed.

HOW ARE YOU SABOTAGING GETTING WHAT YOU WANT?

_____
_____
_____

If you find it difficult to answer the following question, don't be concerned. You may not yet know the "why" of your sabotage, but as you continue in this process of Sabotage Awareness, the answers will come. As we focus on asking the right question, your unconscious will release the information. Your denial system will continue to keep you from knowing until you are ready.

PHASE 3: Why are you sabotaging? What do you fear?

_____
_____
_____

DREAM IT, DO IT, KEEP IT

This is a simple, three-step formula I use to work with people who want to achieve more in their lives.

#1 <u>DREAM IT</u> — Every external goal starts inside our minds and hearts. The first step is to be aware of your dreams, your desires. To write them down on a piece of paper — if you do only this much, you will already be ahead of 97% of the population! If you don't know what your wants or dreams are, answer this question: "If the best happens that can possibly happen for you, what would your career, love-life, health, etc. be like?" Answer this for every important area of your life. There's your <u>dream</u>.

     The next step is, you need to marry your dream of what you want with personal action.

#2 <u>DO IT</u> — this is the action phase of realizing your goals. You need an action plan. "What do I <u>do</u> to make my goals a reality?" "What are the steps?" Write them down as specifically as possible.

_____

_____

_____

#3 <u>KEEP IT</u> — This is the Deserve Level issue. Without permission to keep what I work hard to achieve, I must sabotage it. I can enjoy my achievements and celebrate my victories — or undo them.

I worked with a Sales Director in Mary Kay Cosmetics who had challenges with keeping it. She grew up in a hard-working family of humble origins. She won several Mary Kay cars and national recognition — then sabotaged herself. She suffered from POST-ACHIEVEMENT SABOTAGE — she reached her goals, then stopped selling and recruiting and lost her cars and the success she had achieved. This cycle of striving for the goal, then undermining herself, repeated until she resolved her underlying lack of permission.

Sabotage occurs at every step of the three-step process. At the **"Dream It"** stage, it is never having a goal to strive for. Sabotage at the **"Do It"** stage is not doing what's needed to actualize the specific goal, or PRE-ACHIEVEMENT SABOTAGE. You get side-tracked, find reasons not to produce, etc. Sabotage strategies you might use are "Denial," "Resignation," or "Fatal Flaw."

The sabotage of the **"Keep It"** stage is the "I don't deserve it" feelings. That gets acted out as a POST-ACHIEVEMENT sabotage strategy of "Throwing it Away" or "Settling for Less."

CHAPTER EIGHT
~
DESERVE DILEMMAS

"You gain strength, courage, confidence
by every experience in which you really stop to look
fear in the face...
you must do the thing you think you cannot"
Eleanor Roosevelt

There are several areas of challenge in our Deserve Level that span all of life's choice categories of love, work, health, etc. These Deserve Dilemmas affect all of us to varying degrees of intensity. The three main ones are:

1. Our <u>ability to ask for what we want.</u>
2. The <u>kind</u> and <u>amount of guilt</u> we have.
3. Our <u>ability to focus our time and energy.</u>

These Deserve Dilemmas are programmed by our beliefs and permission from our past. ***Our ability to ASK for what we want is the primary issue in raising our Deserve Level.***

ASK AND RECEIVE

In their book <u>The Aladdin Factor</u>, Jack Canfield and Mark Victor Hansen discuss five barriers to asking:

1.   Ignorance: This breaks into three categories. We don't know what is available and possible. We don't know how to ask for it. We don't know what we want.

2.   Limiting Beliefs: Here's our old friend again (negative self-talk and old, limited beliefs). Some of the common sabotaging beliefs are (a) "If you really loved me I wouldn't have to ask." (b) "If I have to ask for something it is less valuable than if you give it without my asking." (c) "I'm selfish (greedy, bad, etc.) for asking or desiring anything for myself." (d)"My getting something will deprive someone else. There's only a limited supply of (love, money, health, etc.)."

3.   Fears: We all know how these horrible thoughts can stop us from getting what we want.

4.   Low Self-Esteem: It's okay for everyone else to be successful or loved, but I won't ever have it for myself. This is a central core issue in not deserving to have what we want. The self statement is my needs aren't important. Everyone else comes first.

A trinity of negatives make up low self-esteem: (a) A feeling of unworthiness. (b) My needs aren't important. (c) I'm not lovable or likable.

If we could defeat these negatives, most of our life would shine. If we don't feel worthy how can we ever begin to ask? I'm reminded of a story that Cathy, a client of mine, told me about her mother. Cathy had just moved to her first new apartment, and she invited her mother over for her favorite dinner. Cathy spent all day cleaning the house and readying the special meal. She served it and her mother just picked at her food. Cathy asked "What's the matter? I fixed your favorite meal — chicken backs!" Her mom said "Oh, I never really liked chicken backs. I only ate them because they were all that was left after you kids got the white meat." Cathy's mom had grown up in a culture and home that never listened to what she liked or wanted. She was discounted and ignored. She lived a lifetime of never asking for what she desired.

5.   **Pride:** "It's only good if I figure it out myself." "I don't want to ask for help." The feeling that "I Have to do Everything Myself" is the first sign of the Rescuer mentality. It guarantees burn-out and lack of completion. Our internal feeling is pressure to know everything, do it right on the first try or feel humiliated and inadequate.

Asking is a prerequisite to growth and development. The reason our learning curve slows down after age five is we stop asking and being curious about our world.

In *The Aladdin Factor* they suggest a great exercise to restart our asking ability.

START ASKING NOW

At bedtime take a few minutes to get quiet and go through this litany:

- What did I want that I did not ask for today?
- Who could have helped me today if I'd asked?
- Where could I have asked for what I wanted and gotten it today?
- How could I have asked more effectively?

Once you receive an answer, create a new image of yourself actually asking for what you wanted. Visualize yourself asking for it more effectively. See yourself doing it the way you would have liked to have done it had you not been so shy, frightened, prideful or defensive. You will be surprised how readily both the circumstances and the "corrections" will come to you.

What this daily activity does for you is heighten your awareness — which is the first step to all behavioral change. It also programs your unconscious to act more assertively and effectively in the future. Make this a daily ritual until you see your behavior changing.

The second Deserve Dilemma is a sense of **Overriding Guilt.** I'd like to differentiate guilt into two different areas: *Appropriate Guilt* and *Inappropriate or Overriding Guilt.*

Appropriate Guilt is the feeling of concern, worry and/or embarrassment that accompanies the awareness that we've done something inappropriate, like spilling coffee on a friend's new dress, or backing into another car and smashing its door, or stepping on someone's foot. We didn't mean to offend or hurt, but we see and feel the negative outcome that resulted, and we feel bad. Healthy people take responsibility for their actions and make the appropriate amends.

Inappropriate or Overriding Guilt is the pervasive sense that we are to blame, that we are at fault for something that is presented to us. It's the "mea culpa" mentality.

The origin of Inappropriate Guilt is usually parents or other authority figures who used their power as a control device. Inappropriate Guilt is not something we choose, it is inflicted upon us by others. After years of being blamed, judged and even manipulated, we internalize the ability to do it to ourselves and others. Guilt starts in a feeling of self-condemnation after something has happened. The next feeling is the need for punishment.

Guilt is tricky because it is not an emotion, but a thought and a judgment of someone's behavior. We look around for someone to blame or we simply blame ourselves. If we project blame onto others, it is a reflection of our own feelings of low self-esteem. We deny any responsibility for our actions — it is always someone else. We are classic victims. The projection of these negative feelings over time pushes away our family, friends and children.

I worked with a woman who had everything in life going for her — money, health, a successful husband and great children. Her fatal flaw was her need to control and "guilt-trip" the people closest to her. She couldn't take personal responsibility or be straight with her needs or anger. She was a "Spider Woman," weaving webs of guilt and manipulation to insure she would get what she wanted. It took some time, but she sabotaged all her good fortune. She got divorced, lost her health and money, and ran off her children. She died a lonely woman.

Guilt by its very nature creates fear and anxiety and cannot co-exist with loving feelings. As a therapist friend of mine once said, "Scratch guilt and underneath you find anger." We are usually angry at the people who make us feel guilty.

The third Deserve Dilemma has to do with parental permissions that affect our lives in many areas, such as how we use our time and focus our energy. We are either given permission to effectively negotiate these areas or we are subtly instructed in sabotage strategies.

The use of time or the misuse of time is one of our Deserve Level Dilemmas. Procrastination is the thief of time. While appearing to be working hard we can literally be giving our life and income away in small chunks.

Many self-employed people have the experience of doing anything rather than doing the task at hand. Many people have told me that they procrastinate on the most important tasks. They do the more preferred tasks then feel angry and frustrated at not getting the "real" tasks done.

When I was writing this book I was a master of procrastinating. I set aside every Friday morning to write. I'd get up and go to work at about 8:30 a.m., I'd sit at my desk and notice I didn't have any pencils sharpened so I'd do that. Then I'd get my notes in order, the phone would ring and I'd answer it. Now I was ready but I needed a little more hot coffee. On my way back from the kitchen I noticed that all my shoes were out of order in my closet. It only takes a minute to get them in order so... The phone would ring again and then I'd be a little hungry. Got the picture? It's now 10:00 a.m.— I've been "at work" on my book for 1-1/2 hours and I haven't written a word!

Procrastination has been described by a psychologist named Premack. Premack's theory is that procrastination occurs when people gorge themselves on more-preferred activities than the tasks at hand. They become so involved in more-preferred activities that they eventually have no time or energy left for the distasteful tasks or projects. Although these people had been very busy, they had not been productive. To resolve this situation, Premack suggests using preferred activities as rewards. In simple terms, you must do some work on the less-preferred tasks before engaging in the preferred activities. For example, you must work on your sales calls for at least an hour before you decide to go have an ice cream cone as a reward. If you decide to go get the ice cream cone first, you will continue to delay the work on your sales.

DESERVE LEVEL THERAPY

The two most frequent problems people have with increasing their Deserve Level are with their **NEGATIVE BELIEFS** and **LACK OF PERMISSION.** In my private consulting, I work with talented people who have hit the wall of self-sabotage because of these two deadly traps. The questions I ask when someone is stuck in a sales or career rut, ongoing bad relationship or chronic health problem are these:

First, what are you saying to yourself when you start to think about this issue?

I remember a lovely blonde network marketing salesperson named Linda who couldn't make enough money. Before she picked up the phone to call her prospects she said to herself, "They won't want to talk to me. I'll only be bothering them." You can imagine the deflating power of these negative beliefs. She was on the verge of giving up a business she loved because of them.

Bill, a bright energetic man who had worked for a corporation, quit his job and started his own home-based business. As long as he was struggling and having a hard time making ends meet, he felt fine. Eventually his business started becoming very successful. Then the real problems began. He kept telling himself, "I shouldn't be making money if I'm not suffering in the process." His career began to nose dive.

The second question I would ask is, what would your parents think about what you are doing or wanting to do?

Linda had a very specific memory of coming home with all her Girl Scout cookies and asking her father to buy a box. He said he'd buy <u>all</u> her boxes because he didn't want her going door to door bothering the neighbors. Now every time she starts to think about calling her "hot" prospects, she freezes and hears her father's message, "Don't bother the neighbors." That lack of permission puts a halt to her recruiting efforts.

Bill had a different lack of permission. He grew up with a "Martyr" complex. His mother taught him by word and action that to suffer was good and noble and that to enjoy life was bad and wrong. Bill remembers his mom constantly being stressed, deeply sighing through conversations and being so tired she couldn't think straight. His belief was that he had to suffer and give up all of his personal wants and needs to rescue others from the consequences of their choices.

Bill's mother taught him that suffering was a person's lot in life and that he should get used to it. Every time Bill started enjoying his success, he felt guilty — as if somehow he was being disloyal or betraying his mother's messages. Then he faced a hard choice, "Do I remain loyal to my mom's definition of how I should suffer and live my life, or do I give myself permission to work and enjoy my life?"

How do you change these interlocking beliefs and lack of permission and give yourself the New Permissions that can free your life? The first step is to identify specifically the negative beliefs and lack of permission. Then flip the negatives to a positive message. If the negative belief includes a lack of permission, then create a statement that involves both. Linda's example is:

NEGATIVE BELIEF: "I'm bothering people when I call them."

LACK OF PERMISSION: Her dad not wanting her to go to the neighbors' homes because she would be bothering them.

So Linda had both problems: a negative belief and corresponding lack of permission. Her new affirmation said: "I'm easily and confidently sharing my business with many people who are open and enjoy hearing about it." She took the negative belief and corresponding lack of permission and stated them POSITIVELY, and added a good feeling about her new experience.

Bill's new statement was, "I love my mother and I choose to make good money while enjoying my life."

EXERCISE:

My Goal:_____
_____
_____
_____

My Negative Belief About My Goal:_____
_____
_____
_____

My Lack of Permission About My Goal:_____
_____
_____
_____

My <u>NEW</u> Self Statement (flip the Negative around to
the Positive and write down your new permission):
_____
_____
_____
_____
_____

~~~

STOP
SELF-SABOTAGE

❋❋❋❋❋❋❋❋❋❋❋❋❋❋❋❋❋❋❋❋❋❋❋❋❋

PART TWO: GETTING OUT OF YOUR OWN WAY

❋❋❋❋❋❋❋❋❋❋❋❋❋❋❋❋❋❋❋❋❋❋❋❋❋

The action steps to stop self-sabotage and up your deserve level are:

SELF-TALK – changing the chat in your head to focus on positive, life-affirming goals.

SELF-RELEASE – getting out the negative feelings that most of use to contain and depress ourselves.

SELF-NURTURING – this is learning to be self-accepting, even when things are going wrong. Developing the ability to turn self-criticism to self-nurturing in stressful situations.

SELF-SUPPORT – the art of creating an emotional safety net for ourselves with loyal friends, supportive work environments and loving families.

All of these are meant to be used together to stop your sabotages and deserve the best.

CHAPTER NINE

~

SELF-TALK

"Each man (woman) holds between his hands
a silence that he wants to fulfill,
so he fills it with his dreams.

"If you can't commit to something big,
commit to something small."
Merle Shain, <u>When Lovers Are Friends</u>

Self-Talk is what you say in your own mind about yourself and the world.

There is a chatterer in your head that talks to you, day in and day out, about what you can do and have and be. These messages can be helpful or can greatly inhibit what happens to you. You are creating your own reality by the tape you play to yourself.

Here is the problem: most Self-Talk is at an unconscious level. The very programs that are running you are often outside of your conscious awareness.

It is hard to understand the unconscious mind because no scientific data exists as to its existence and location. We only know it exists by its influence on our lives.

In any major conflict between the conscious and unconscious minds, the unconscious triumphs.

Basic feelings and needs reside in the unconscious. Our early life decisions and beliefs shape our choices and destiny.

The unconscious mind cannot make a distinction between fantasy and fact. If a person repeats over and over, "I'm shy," "I can't make cold calls," "I'm not pretty," the unconscious mind accepts it as reality, no matter what the objective truth is.

We constantly listen to this dialogue, and through its repetition we create our reality.

AFFIRMATIONS

Everybody has had the experience of energy following thought. Remember the last time you woke up in a bad mood and told yourself it was going to be a rotten day? Proved yourself right, didn't you?

Our reality is what we create by how we define our life experiences. The classic psychological test of an optimist or pessimist is the half glass of water. Is it half full or half empty? Our perception creates our reality. Or as a comic once said, "I know my glass is half empty, I just want to know who's been drinking it!"

Our Self-Talk is made up of affirmations. Affirmations are statements we make about our behavior, feelings and self-worth, both to ourselves and others — statements so repetitive that we don't even notice them.

Some people mistakenly believe that affirmations are only positive statements. In reality, affirmations can be either negative or positive. Statements such as, "I'm always late," or "I'm a good financial planner," or "Attractive women never like me," are all affirmations.

If sabotaging self-talk is what you have been affirming to yourself, you've been creating a negative outcome. Now is the time to compose messages you would rather affirm in your own mind, both conscious and unconscious.

By using the powerful tool that is **purposeful self-talk,** you can turn unconscious limitations into a new vision of reality.

VISUALIZATION

Visualization is a technique that uses vivid mental images as a way of improving performance and influencing outcome.

To make your affirmation even more powerful, allow yourself to visualize the desired outcome as you write or listen to the affirmation. Cut out a magazine illustration, or take a photograph, depicting the things you want.

Whether it is a boat, an elegant home or gorgeous car, a happy relationship, or a serene countenance, concentrating on an image will help to reinforce the words.

Put the picture on your bathroom mirror or your refrigerator or your dashboard. Every time you look at it you will be reminding yourself that this is what you want.

To be effective, affirmations and visualzation need to be combined with action towards the goal. You can't just passively visualize a desired outcome while doing nothing toward it and hope to achieve the results you want. Effective visualization needs to be combined with specific skills and active involvement.

The pictures we make in our minds can either help us get what we want or undermine our attempts. Joe wanted to meet attractive women. He faithfully did affirmations about being with and enjoying an attractive companion, but nothing was happening. When asked about his accompanying visualizations, he answered, "I can't really see anything about her except that she is bored and doesn't want to be with me. Then I see myself standing alone and feeling miserable." His negative pictures were sabotaging his positive affirmations.

After he began visualizing a woman turning toward him with delight on her face, his whole attitude about himself with women changed. Since the real issue is to find yourself first, and then relationships will follow. It is not surprising that he made a connection with a lovely woman just a few weeks later.

Get clear on the things you want and it is amazing how they then show up. Again, it is not magic. It is a change in perception and in what kind of nonverbal messages you send out to others.

Peter Thomas and his success exemplify the visualization/affirmation process. Peter was

Chairman of the Board and CEO of Century 21 of Canada. He started the company from zero, and when he sold it he had six thousand employees.

Peter is a firm believer in the power of your own beliefs to create your reality. He carries with him, in his daily organizer, pictures of what he wants. When he opens a page you can see his 65-foot yacht, his airplane and his new Rolls-Royce.

All of his "toys" he has acquired by affirming, visualizing and organizing his life to meet his chosen goals.

Affirmation and visualization techniques have become commonplace in the world of athletics, medicine and sales.

The U.S. Olympics sports psychology experts have been using VMBR (visuo-motor-behavior rehearsal) since the early '70s. From experience we know that practice can improve performance. What athletes have learned is that some of that needed practice can go on in our minds.

VMBR involves fifteen to twenty minutes of relaxation followed by mental rehearsal in which you see yourself doing your desired behavior as well as you can do it. You see yourself jumping the moguls perfectly, or running the fastest mile even in wet weather, or bobsledding down the hill in the best time.

For challenge and variety you can change the scenes or the difficulty. What is important is the mental practice and repetitive experience of success.

Studies have shown that the athletes who use VMBR do improve their performances.

Similar visualization techniques are being used in the medical field. At the Cancer Counseling and Research Center started by Carl and Stephanie Simonton, therapists train cancer patients to visualize their cancer as loose, unorganized cells, and their immune system as healthy, powerful cells doing battle with and defeating the cancer cells. The process is repeated three times a day for twenty minutes at a time, with attention to concrete visualization of the powerful white cells.

This psychological therapy does not replace conventional medical interventions, but rather augments them.

The procedure, innovative when it was introduced eighteen years ago, is now widely replicated. There have been remissions in predicted terminal cases, and in every case the patient has gained a sense of involvement, so that he is not just a "case" to the medical profession, but is himself part of the treatment. One of the most devastating aspects of cancer is the helplessness the patient often feels. By becoming involved in the treatment, patients feel a renewed sense of power to influence the outcome of their illness.

Many practitioners in the visualization field have found that the best results come from the most detailed and specific images. Sarah, a cancer patient with an interest in the Renaissance, saw her cancer as barbarians attacking her castle and her white blood cells as valiant white knights fighting for the holy cause. Her cancer went into remission and has remained there for three years.

In the very different field of sales training, I use visualization techniques to help promote salespeople's self-motivation. I have them place pictures of what they want on their desks: the new car, trimmer body, new house, and so on. Every time they make a sales call or pick up the phone, their visual goal is in front of them.

A helpful technique is to write out your sales goal for the month and post it on your desk, or on your telephone. Every time you are working or talking with a client, you are sub-vocalizing your goal.

Another visualization/affirmation tool that is beneficial for sales professionals is what I call "pre-game." My idea for this technique came from the movie "Big," with Tom Hanks. As the creative director of a toy company, he is preparing for the big meeting in his office. He's standing there holding a bunch of pencils in his hand and throwing them into the ceiling. His secretary interrupts and he says, "Don't disturb me, I'm in pre-game."

Pre-game is where we visualize the outcome we want before we go through the process. We see the new customer relationship going well before we even meet the prospect. It's taking five minutes before the sales call to predict a positive outcome.

Using these behavioral-rehearsal strategies, just close your eyes and run the movie of what you want to happen.

Sondra Ray, in her book I Deserve Love, makes excellent suggestions for writing affirmations. She suggests that you:

√ Be specific and vivid in descriptions.
√ See them happen.
√ Write them in positive language.
√ Write them twenty times a day.
√ Write them daily for three weeks.

When writing, use the *first person present tense*, as if what you want is happening right now.

AFFIRMATIONS EXERCISE:

Think about one thing you want, and write it down in the first person, present tense.

"I am now... _____

_____

_____

_____

_____

_____

_____

Examples:

"...making a hundred thousand dollars a year."
"...enjoying a relationship with a loving, charming person who appreciates me."
"...healthy, physically fit and more alive."
"...more deeply religious, spiritually developed, happy in my life."

You need to write or say your affirmation twenty times a day for twenty-one days to implant that information into your brain. It takes that many repetitions and that much frequency to implant your new belief. Remember, your old negative programs have been getting reinforced daily for decades — it only makes sense to give your mind a concentrated dose of the new message.

Candy Costello, a beautiful, capable Mary Kay Sales Director, sent me her laundry list of wants. She has wisely covered several areas of her life:

"I am married to a loving, sensitive, financially secure Christian man who cherishes me."

"God has given me a spirit of power and love, and a sound, disciplined mind. My God is stronger than any adversity that might come my way today."

"I am enjoying the benefits of a $5,000 monthly income... Tithing $500 and saving $1,000."

What's your list? What do you deeply desire to have in your life?

There are several forms your affirmation can take. You can **write** the statement twenty times every day. If you prefer, you can make a tape of yourself saying the affirmation twenty times, and then **listen** to it as you get dressed in the morning or as you drive to and from work. (Some people find it more effective to have someone else's voice saying the affirmation, utilizing the "authority effect.")

The important thing is consistency. It will not work if you write/hear the affirmation a few times today and then not again till next month.

If you hear a negative statement in response to your affirmation, ignore it and return with more force to the positive statement. If the negative reply persists, use it as a clue to discover further negative self-talk that is persisting deeper in your unconscious mind.

The brain has 4 states of consciousness:
- BETA   Wide awake, alert consciousness
- ALPHA   Relaxed and creative state
- THETA   Where we usually fall asleep
- DELTA   Deep sleep

We go through these four states daily. To use affirmations and visualizations to best advantage, we need to program them in at both the Beta and Alpha states. For best results, say/hear/see your affirmations when you are in Beta (energetic and wide awake) and again in Alpha (relaxed, creative, intuitive).

Accessing your Alpha state needs to occur in a protected environment. You are changing to a "twilight" state of consciousness. Obviously, you should not be driving, and you should be free from the likelihood of interruptions.

You can create an <u>Alpha Access Tape</u> that will help you reach the desired level of relaxation that creates optimum suggestibility.

ALPHA ACCESS TAPE

This is a self-hypnosis technique that you can use to help enter your affirmations into your most receptive mental state. To make this tape you will need only a recorder, pencil and paper.

First write down your affirmations, exactly as you want them to be experienced. Now either get a friend to tape the following transcript, reading in a calm deliberate voice, or you do it if you want your own voice to be the one you hear.

Get very comfortable — stretch out, keep your feet straight. I want you to pretend that you're on a beach and you're sitting there in the sun. It is a very pleasant beach. It's not too hot. The sun is warm and you're looking at the water. The water is blue and crystal clear, easily washing up to the shore. As you are looking at the water, you are breathing very deeply. As the water comes up to the shore, you are inhaling, watching the water toward you. As the water goes back out to sea, you're exhaling. Watch the waves and enjoy this kind of circular process. Feel yourself inhale while the waves come up to the shore, and feel yourself exhale as the waves go back to sea.

You feel very comfortable and relaxed, very unstressed. I want you to take a short journey with me. We're going to get on an elevator at the 10th floor; we are going down to the 1st floor. When the doors open at the 1st floor, we are going to walk into one of your favorite rooms. It can be a room where you already live, or this can be a room that you just think about and fantasize. But it has to be some place that feels especially good and restful to you.

Walk into the elevator and look up and see the floor that says 10. You are watching the floors as you descend, 9, and 8. You are feeling more and more relaxed. 7, 6, 5. You are feeling more and more comfortable and relaxed. 4, 3, 2. More and more relaxed. And now you are at the 1st floor. The doors open. You walk into your favorite room. This is the most comfortable and pleasant place you can imagine.

Look around this room. I want you to select a chair or a couch and sit down on it. See the couch. Feel yourself sitting down. Look at the walls. What is on the wall? Just enjoy that room in your imagination.

As you sit there, listen to your affirmations. As you listen, I am going to read them to you. Allow yourself to believe you can have them. Open up your Deserve Level and allow yourself to receive.

You are feeling relaxed, comfortable, happy with the thought of getting more of what you deserve.

Now I want you to get up from your chair and walk back to the elevator. See yourself get on the elevator at the ground floor and go slowly up to the tenth floor. First floor, 2, 3, you are feeling relaxed, happy, 4, 5, 6, feeling more alert and confident, 7, 8, 9, feeling positive and alert. And the tenth floor. The doors open and your eyes open and you are back in this room, awake and alert.

Play this tape whenever you want to focus on your goals. Do it at least once a day for three weeks, so your unconscious can absorb the material.

The outcome of affirmations can be attested to by people who committed to using them. There was a married couple, John and Marsha, who had become so irritated with each other that they were contemplating divorce. Marsha decided to affirm:

"John and I are getting along great. We love each other, have kind and positive communication, and enjoy great sex."

Every morning Marsha would play this tape while she was putting on her makeup. John thought the whole thing was mumbo-jumbo, but every morning while he was shaving at the next sink, he was listening to her affirmation.

A few weeks later Marsha said to their marriage counselor, "I don't know what's happened, but John and I are treating each other nicely." John still thought the process was hocus-pocus, but he said thoughtfully, "I guess hearing that every morning and thinking it might be possible IS influencing me."

Right now you can probably sing radio and TV jingles from the '60s or '50s or '40s. You hear certain melodies and you can sing verbatim the words that accompanied them. Unconsciously we absorbed that material until it became part of us, and then we repeated it back to ourselves to complete the loop.

Affirmations and visualization allow you to CHOOSE to take in what is in your own best interest.

BETA ACCESS TIPS (wide-awake state)

1. Find a reasonably contemplative time to write/ hear your affirmations. Dressing, driving, unwinding after your day — these are good times. It is unwise to listen while you are doing some strenuous task. Choose a time when you are calm and quiet and have at least ten minutes to devote to it.

2. Focus your energy and concentration into saying your affirmations the entire twenty repetitions each time, rather than five in the morning, five more at lunch and so on.

3. The more often you say/listen to the twenty repetitions, the faster the information will be absorbed. Twice a day is better than once a day, but once a day is often enough to accomplish the desired outcome.

4. Figure out how you would sabotage the reaching of your goal, and then structure the affirmation so that it cures the sabotage message in advance. If you want to quit smoking but fear that you will gain weight, say something like "I am an elegant, slim non-smoker."

5. Use a positive statement rather than a negative one. Say, "I am an elegant, slim non-smoker," rather than "I am repulsed by the nastiness of cigarettes. I hate that I have such a vile habit."

6. Concentrate on one to three affirmations at a time. If you have a long list, work on just one, two or three at a time. Taking on more than you can reasonably handle might be a way you have sabotaged yourself in the past.

7. Recycling: as you get each thing you want, you can create a new affirmation about something else you want.

The more sensory channels you use, the better. Some people like to set their affirmations to music — they can sing them, chant them, listen to them, even dance to them.

I did affirmations for five years about finishing this book. I think I wrote more affirmations than chapters. Every time I would get discouraged that I wasn't done, I'd ask myself, "Do I still want this goal to happen?" The answer was always "yes," so I'd reinvest in doing my affirmations Finally, when I finished this book, I refocused my affirmations to a new goal.

I've taught affirmations/visualizations seminars around the world for the last ten years. Every time I conduct a seminar for a group, I ask them to let me know when they reach their goals. I have had many happy phone calls and letters attesting to the fact that affirmations work if you just do them.

This is a small sampling of the "good news" letters I have received. For many more answered prayers, see Chapter 14, "I Got It!"

On an unusual-looking postcard from Malaysia: *"Dear Pat — I met you at a Century 21 convention. I promised to send you a card if I was able to make my trip. Well, here I am in Kota Kinabalu, Malaysia, Borneo. This has been great — worth selling houses for this experience."*

Elaine High
Century 21 Pleasant
Valley Properties
Camarillo, California

Susan, a highly successful businesswoman in her mid-thirties, had a particularly interesting sabotage. Having fun was a high priority to her, and she was only attracted to men who could be very entertaining. The problem was they were all under-achievers or unsuccessful in their business lives, and she ended up being their financial supporter — which eventually wasn't much fun!

She had an unconscious belief that a man could not be successful in business and be fun (although she was). She went to parties and ended up liking the waiters and ignoring all her business associates.

She decided to do an affirmation that said, "I am with a fun, successful man who is a good communicator." Within six weeks Steve showed up, handsome, fun and very successful.

Vicki Knight, General Sales Manager of KPLX-KLIF radio, Dallas, Texas: Vickie's affirmation was, "I'm experiencing a loving and supportive relationship with a wonderful and understanding man — who loves to dance!"

Vicki was re-entering the single scene after a traumatic divorce and feeling all the normal apprehensions of that process.

In her words, "I wrote my affirmation in my appointment book and read it or wrote it every day. I went home for vacation in July and met Dan Swain. We went dancing and have been dancing together ever since!" Vicki and Dan were married several months after their first dance.

How about a career dream being visualized and created? Marie Kordus (KPWR in Los Angeles) was interested in advancing to general sales manager of her radio station. She affirmed and intently focused on her goals, and within months she had the job she had wished for.

Marie stayed in her job for several years, then decided that she wanted to be General Manager. She used the same affirmation techniques for her new job, and after two months, she became the General Manager of KPWR. Two career advances using the same affirmation process.

In my work I have found that most people take more time balancing their checkbooks or planning their grocery lists than they do in writing down what they want for a relationship, career or health goal. We make lists for everything from laundry to Christmas presents, yet we don't make a list of what we want in our lives.

You had little or no control over the programming of your earlier life that brought you to this stage, but you can take control of the rest of your life if you choose. To paraphrase Thornton Wilder in The Bridge of San Luis Rey,

"We either live and die by chance, or we live and die by a plan."

You can choose. Through repetition of affirmations and visualizations, you can reprogram yourself to a more abundant life, however you define it.

CHAPTER TEN

~

SELF-RELEASE: TELLING YOURSELF THE TRUTH ABOUT YOUR FEELINGS

"When you become lonely and you become afraid, all the answers you will ever need will be found within yourself. Do not look so frantically out into the world for the answers to your questions. Look within and ask yourself, 'Am I being faithful to my own truth?' Losing that faith is the only real sin."

Lynn Andrews, <u>The Woman of Wyrrd</u>

Every self-help book agrees positive Self-Talk is necessary, but why isn't it enough? Why doesn't everybody who reads a positive-thinking book get what he wants?

To answer that question, look again at **SELF-CONFIDENCE** and **SELF-ESTEEM.** Each is necessary but not sufficient.

The same is true of **THOUGHTS** and **FEELINGS**. Changing Self-Talk from negative to positive is a process based on chosen thoughts. The other part that can keep us stuck, no matter how fervently we follow a self-help program, is our unresolved feelings. In the process of increasing your

Deserve Level, you need to get your feelings as clear and authentic as you can. When you have learned to integrate your thoughts and your feelings so they are congruent, honoring both, you have complete permission to have what you want. Most of us do not like to acknowledge our "negative" feelings. We would like it if they were gone — if we never felt mad or sad or frustrated or hurt or upset again. We would like those painful feelings just to go away, but that is not how the mind works.

You have to express your feelings to be able to release them and get free of their negative impact. Then, and only then, can positive Self-Talk find a place to get in and stay in. Otherwise, your negative feelings will do a seek-and-destroy mission on your positive Self-Talk.

There are two important premises about feelings:
1) Feelings are "facts."
2) There are only two ways feelings can be expressed — out (released) or in (contained).

FEELINGS ARE FACTS

Whatever you feel is immutable fact to your Unconscious — it is not up for debate. Yet, because most of us have a hard time accepting our feelings, we deny them or tell ourselves they are "wrong." When you say to yourself, "I shouldn't feel that way; that isn't a nice way to feel," or, "I really don't feel attracted to this fabulous man," your Unconscious gets confused. It has a different set of "facts."

In this culture most of us were cut off from our anger. We grew up hearing, "Don't raise your voice to me. Go to your room and don't come out till you can put on a nice face." We have been taught to tell ourselves we do not feel anger, which really means we do not acknowledge or express it.

The result: we store it in our bodies or convert it to depression.

The American Psychiatric Association now asserts that ordinary low-grade depression is no longer a psychiatric disorder because <u>everybody has it</u>. What a comment on our society! It is now normal in America to be depressed. As a culture we have so conspired not to feel, not to express, that all those unacknowledged feelings have turned inward and depressed us.

Anger is the road to your passion. It is your vehicle to be able to take a stand for yourself.

To the extent that you deny anger, you deny life.

Perhaps there were other feelings you were not allowed in your childhood — sadness or fear or hurt. To whatever extent you become able to express them, you will give yourself back the life energy that you have blocked.

Tara is an example of the "Too Nice" syndrome. Growing up, she went to a very strict school. "Every time I would try to say something that they didn't like, the nuns would tell me 'You're bad and stupid.

104

You don't know anything,' she told me." Later Tara worked for a major corporation. Passed over many times for a promotion or recognition, she became a Rescuer to reduce her pain. Instead of admitting her anger, she became nicer to cover the feelings.

The problem was, the more she gave, the less she felt validated. What she really needed to do was protest. By not saying anything she was tacitly agreeing to it.

As Tara said, "I didn't feel I deserved anything, so I tried to be nicer, hoping that would work." Because her basic needs for personhood weren't being acknowledged, she didn't feel she had a right to be treated well. Once she started protesting these personal discounts, then her depression lifted, and she started to truly feel alive.

THERE ARE ONLY TWO WAYS FEELINGS CAN GO: IN OR OUT.

If they are not allowed out, they have to go in. The result can be psychological or stress-related physical symptoms or diseases — headaches, neckaches, backaches, cancer, heart problems, ulcers.

The challenge is to learn effective ways to get your feelings out — not to rail at your boss or your wife, or in any other way hurt yourself, but to find other, neutral ways to get them out and not keep them internalized.

We usually see only two alternatives: to contain our feelings or dump them on someone else. There is a third way. Release them in a controlled way by intentionally crying, yelling, or acting them out.

The key is to express them and not hurt yourself or anyone else in the process.

This is the missing part of our emotional survival training. In self-release the single most important issue is to release, not contain. If you feel hurt, cry. If you feel angry, express it. The challenge is to find a way to express it that doesn't compound your problem.

Later in this section I'll be delineating several "Release Valves" to aid in self-expression.

WHATEVER YOU HAVE NOT BEEN ABLE TO DO IS WHAT YOU MUST LEARN TO DO

The challenge is to be authentic with your feelings and not get them crossed. In this culture, boys are taught to deny their pain, so instead of acknowledging hurt, they get mad. Women are taught to deny anger, so instead of getting mad, they get hurt.

A recent study at the University of Michigan revealed that women who express their anger live longer than those who don't. Three times as many women who suppressed their anger died during the course of the study as those who spoke right up. What an incentive to learn to express your true feelings!

To the extent that you are prohibited, you are trapped. To be fully human, you must allow yourself spontaneity across the full spectrum of humanness.

GRIEF

All of us have had losses in our lives, yet we often have not allowed ourselves to fully heal through the grief process. This is true for any loss in your life — love, friends, health, jobs, marriage. Yet, most people do not understand the necessity of moving through the grief process. They block themselves at some point in it by discounting or denying their feelings.

To help you know where you may be unfinished at some stage of a grief in your life, here is the progression which grief takes, explained more fully by Elizabeth Kubler-Ross in her monumental book, On Death and Dying.

1.   **Denial.** "I can't believe this is happening!" My marriage is not failing. My mother is not terminally ill.

2.   **Bargaining.** "What can I do so we won't get divorced?" "What do I have to do to keep this job?" "Lord, if you'll just let her live, I'll go to church every Sunday for the rest of my life." Like the magical thinking of childhood, you are in a stage in which you believe that something you DO can change the loss.

3.   **Sadness.** You let yourself feel your pain and loss. You let yourself cry. Your heart can literally ache during this stage. The feeling can come and go. You can be driving down the street feeling OK, and a song comes on the radio and you're destroyed. You

can be in a business meeting and hear someone say something that reminds you of a poignant moment, and internally you collapse.

When you are going through these rapid changes you can feel crazy. You aren't crazy. You are just grieving.

4.   Depression. This is a kind of numbness. You don't care any more. You may sleep a lot, find it hard to get up in the morning, or you may have insomnia. You are not motivated even to see your friends. You lose the luster of life.

5.   Anger. You get mad about the loss. Perhaps you are angry at the person who died. You have been left, and you did not want the person to leave. In marriages that are divorcing this can be a very painful, accusing stage, and can go on for a long time.

6.   Resolution. The pain has at last been handled. You can talk about it, feel it, without being demolished. This is the all-important stage of forgiveness — forgiveness of self and the other for all the pain. Then there can be a returning to the belief that no one intended the pain.

Wherever you are stuck in the grieving process, that is the place you must release. If you are still angry at your ex-spouse, then you need to release the anger and forgive. The anger only bonds you two in negative ways.

Everyone in this culture goes through grief, sometimes multiple griefs simultaneously. Obviously, if you have two or three going on at the same time, it is going to further diminish your energy.

If your feelings are not backing up what you want — if you do not have the energy to focus on what you want and deserve — you will not be able to accomplish it.

It has been said by several of my colleagues that all therapy is grief work — grieving for the lost dreams, unanswered hopes, and wounded child feelings in all of us.

SELF-RELEASE AND SELF-ESTEEM

The only way to build self-esteem is to have your feelings and your self-worth acknowledged. If that did not happen when you were a child, it needs to happen now.

**Self-release is the hardest
issue in Deserve Level.**

Positive Self-Talk, learning to say nice things to yourself, is considerably easier. Feelings are much dearer and deeper than thoughts. You are the person who can make it happen, and you begin by honoring your feelings.

DIAGNOSTIC EXERCISE:

Take a moment now to write about your unresolved feelings. State what they are, who is involved in them, and what you tell yourself that keeps you from releasing them.

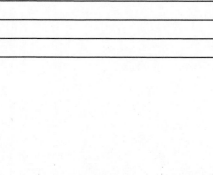

TAKE ACTION!

~

RELEASE VALVES: EXERCISES FOR POSITIVE EXPRESSION OF UNRESOLVED FEELINGS

The challenge here is to get out all those feelings that are causing your grief and release the bondage they are keeping you in. If you feel silly or embarrassed as you do them, remind yourself that it's the best way to get rid of the negatives.

GET OFF MY BACK!

This exercise is done standing up with your knees slightly bent. Your arms are held up and bent at the elbow so your hands are facing each other.

Now, think about the last time someone really made you angry. Think about what they said, focus on your feelings about them and their statements.

Pull back your arms as if you were rowing a boat, and with feeling say, "GET OFF MY BACK!" Keep doing it, at least ten times, until you feel a release from your angry feelings. No wimping out — really try and get them off your back!

TENNIS RACKET RELEASE

When some people are really angry, they like to hit things. Often what happens is that they contain and contain until they explode and hit whatever is handy. I know a man who lost control in a rage and smashed his fist into a glass coffee table, ending up with 22 stitches.

That is uncontrolled hitting. The tennis racket release is a wonderful, intentional alternative. All it takes is an old tennis racket and a bed or pile of big pillows.

Mentally place the person you are angry at beside the bed, in a good vantage point to watch you. Now hit the pillows with all your power and tell the person what you are angry about. Keep it simple, one sentence or two at the most. "I'm furious that you left me." "I'm angry that you don't want to have sex." Really get into it, say anything you want, and completely release it by whomping the bed with the tennis racket. Find a satisfying rhythm between the words and the racket smacks.

The feeling at the end of this kind of experience is great. Every time I do it I feel emotionally cleansed. And here's the good news: the other person doesn't even know what I've said. I have released my anger without hurting myself or anyone else, and now I can be rational with the person I'm angry with.

KILL SOMEONE IN YOUR SHOWER (THE "PSYCHO" RELEASE)

This release is performed in the comfort of your own shower. Turn on the water and get your wash cloth and soap. Now, think of all the negative things you want to say to the person you're angry with. Picture them there and say anything you want. Throw the wash cloth, yell, cuss, toss the soap at them. Then wash off the rest of your anger and step out physically and emotionally clean.

CLOWN YOUR WAY THROUGH

Many people find a good release in laughing away their tensions. If that appeals to you, another technique when you're feeling sad or angry is to laugh it away. One helpful way is with the clown technique.

If you've had a bad day and are frustrated and upset, get in your car and pull out your "clown nose." Put in on and casually drive home waving at people as you pass them. You can't stay in a funk for very long with a clown nose on your face.

TEA AND SYMPATHY

If you're feeling depressed or low, one of the best strategies is real contact with people you love. Your best friend, a close work associate, a family member — someone you can predict will be kind and care about your pain.

Share with your friend as deeply as you can what you are really feeling and let them give back their love and concern. If they shift into advice, remind them that what you want is a caring, listening ear — sympathy and support.

CHAPTER ELEVEN
~
COMMUNICATION AND CONNECTION

"I think that what we're (all) seeking is an experience
of being alive, so that our life experiences...
will have resonances within our most innermost being,
so that we actually feel the rapture of being alive."
Joseph Campbell, <u>The Power of Myth</u>

We have relationships everywhere — at work, friendships, at home — and when things are not going well in some of your relationships, communication is often a major factor. How does communication in relationships get bogged down?

The single most destructive interaction in human relations is what has been called the **RESCUE TRIANGLE**. It occurs in intimate relationships, in the workplace, in management. It is a particular form of negative communication patterns and role assumptions, based on unhealthy dependency, which keeps all its players frustrated and resentful.

Here is how the triangle looks:

PERSECUTOR		RESCUER
	▽	
	VICTIM	

1. **Rescuers** are people who are over-responsible. They give 90% and get back 10%. They do not say NO when they don't want to do things, because they are afraid of appearing selfish. They see as their NEED to give and nurture and take care of other people. They do not ask for what they want, because they see it as their JOB to be there for others, ever-ready and ever-responsive. They don't set firm boundaries for the same reasons.

Most of us have been trained that it is more blessed to give than to receive. The problem with being in a determined Rescuer position is that it is obligatory. Rescuers do not see an acceptable alternative. Often they are not giving because they want to, but because they think they SHOULD.

Rescuers tell themselves, "No matter what I feel, what I want or need, what is going on with me, I have no right to myself. I am here to cater to and give to you." "You" is virtually everyone: husband, wife, corporation, children, parents, friends.

2.   **Victims** are people who are under-responsible. They invite and need Rescuers to tell them what to do and rescue them. They tend to be passive and don't know what they want.   They tend not to take responsibility for themselves, nor indeed for what they create in their world. They look to other people to make things right for them. They have a sense of being powerless, unable to do things or create positive outcomes in their lives. They believe life has victimized them. They feel helpless and hopeless and look to assign blame for their feelings on someone else. "They made me ..." is their emotional litany.

Each of us is sometimes a true victim — that is, caught in a situational bind not of our own making. A friend really can find that his battery has died overnight, and will call and ask you for a ride. If, however, he has a different broken-car reason to call you every day, he is playing in the Rescue Triangle. He is not taking responsibility for getting his own car in order — or his life, or his financial condition, or whatever "emergency" he creates to "need" you to rescue him.

Let's observe a Rescue Triangle in action at a family dinner table (which is often where it originates). This scenario happened every night in my family around the important issue of iced tea.

I put sugar in my iced tea. Dad, coming from Persecutor position, glowers and says, putting me in the Victim role, "You are going to die of diabetes. There is diabetes in this family, and you are going to die of it."

Because this happens every night, I open my science book and say "But we're studying about diabetes in school, Dad. It says here that it takes a lot more than just sugar to cause diabetes."

Dad totally discounts my source and continues to rant at me about the sugar in my tea. He also tells me not to get smart with him.

And who comes in at this point? Mom, in the Rescuer Position. "There, there, honey, it's OK, your Dad doesn't mean to be angry." Dad turns on her and says, "That's the trouble with this family, there is NO DISCIPLINE, and it's YOUR FAULT!" Mom can now play Victim.

I come back in and say to Mom, "Come on, Mom, let's go play Scrabble together." I rescue her and we leave.

Who won? Nobody! We bought a ticket and took the ride around the entire Rescue Triangle, and everybody was left with bad feelings.

The irony of the Rescue Triangle is that all people can, at some time or another, play every position. If you rescue long enough, you become a victim. You also can move into the role of Persecutor.

That bears repeating. ***Once you buy a ticket to play Rescue, you eventually go around the whole cycle.***

This is a relationship based on need. Victims need Rescuers (and vice versa). So, what happens when Victims start feeling better about themselves? One of two things. Maybe they say to the Rescuer,

117

"Thanks so much, but I don't need you any more. I will always remember how you were there for me during and after my divorce, but I am going off now to marry Harry/Sally." Or else they might get angry and say, "I never needed you in the first place. You're driving me crazy. Bug off!" In other words, they can get angry, which enables them to play Persecutor.

3.   Persecutors are people who are angry, frustrated, fed up. They are frequently Rescuers who have had it and flipped into the Persecutor position. When a Rescuer moves into Persecutor she/he might say, "I'm mad at you, I've had it with you. After all I've done for you, how can you treat me like this?" They are often quite justified in their anger, because they have over-given and over-done.

Now, ask yourself: What happens inside nice people after they persecute? Exactly: **They feel guilty!** Guilt then builds a bridge from Persecutor back to Rescuer, and they get to go on another ride. "I was so awful, why did I act like that. This time I am going to be really nice. I'll give even more, delay my own gratification and take care of that other person."

Rescue is the most predominate game of negative communication played in this culture. It is rampant, not only with couples and families, but in the marketplace. Think of how a lot of corporations are run — to say nothing of small-shop entrepeunerships — and you will be able to write your own scenarios to illustrate the Rescue game.

That is not to say that all giving is a game of Rescue. When you want to give to somebody, as long as you take responsibility for the giving and take care of yourself in the process, you are all right. Even then, however, notice if you are the giver a disproportionate amount of the time.

Rescuers are doing it out of a sense of obligation, because they think they have to, as if it were their consecrated life work.

Ironically, it is the person you give too much to who ends up leaving you for someone else (in business or romance), or at the very least exploiting you. If a real estate agent gives 150% to a prospective buyer, he is exactly the one who will end up buying through another agent. It is the long-suffering super-givers who often get left in mid-life for another woman/man. If you play rescuer, you will end up as victim.

How do you avoid taking the ride?
1)   Know what you want and how to ask for it.
2)   Do not give more than your fair share. Sometimes 60/40, but NOT 90/10.
3)   Ask for people to give back. This is true in any relationship, personal or business. If they don't, they are not invested in the relationship, and you need to know that. In sales, there are customers none of us can afford to have. They are the ones that sap your time and energy and never give back by buying. Or if they do buy they are endlessly demanding.

4)   Remember that good relationships are a dance for two. If you are taking all the steps, the other person cannot dance with you. Take a step, and then wait and let your partner take a step. Give her or him a chance — don't preempt his move with your impatience or your impulse to over-give.

5)   In personal relationships, do not allow yourself to fall in love with someone's potential. Rocks have potential! If you do, chances are you have found an under-responsible Victim for you to Rescue ("surely the love of a good woman will turn him around/open him up to intimacy/ show him how good life can be"). Fall in love with reality.

6)   If you find yourself really indignant or resentful (at a lover, friend, boss), notice that the same principles apply. You have probably been setting yourself up to play the role of Rescuer/Martyr. A clue is your response to a phone message from them. If you hear it and go, "Oh no, not him!" — BINGO! you are in the Rescue Triangle.

7)   Say NO to what you really do not want to do. It will not turn out well if you say "Yes" when you mean "No."

8)   Set your boundaries and don't change them.

JUST SAY NO

Ann tells a story that rings familiar bells with many of us: She returned home from a week-long business trip, worn out, and was talking with her husband about plans for the evening. She said, "I'm exhausted. All I want to do is be entertained. Let's go to a movie."

He said, "OK." She went on to suggest a funny movie she had read about and once again he said, "OK."

Sitting in the movie, Ann was happy as a lark with her popcorn in one hand, a Diet Coke in the other, just enjoying the experience. Then she began to pick up negative vibes from her husband. She ignored them, hoping they would go away.

After the movie they went out to eat. All through dinner he was very quiet. Finally she said, "What's wrong?" and he responded, "Nothing." Finally she said, "What is the problem, what have I done that is irritating you?"

He said, "I didn't want to go to the movies, and I really didn't want to go to <u>that</u> movie!"

"Why did you?"

"I wanted to make sure you had a good evening!"

How many of us have tried to make sure someone else is happy and done something we didn't want to do? And in the process, made everyone miserable.

The Rescue Ride starts out with the best of intentions and blows up in our faces.

BOUNDARIES

Boundaries are the limits to which you are willing to go. We show healthy boundaries to others when we decline to be exploited.

Set your boundaries and stick with them. That means setting boundaries within yourself, because these old behavior patterns can be addictive.

Communication is not just inter-personal (you with others), it is also intra-personal (you with yourself). You can be kind, but firm, with yourself about not allowing your old patterns to keep running you, particularly if they keep hurting you.

I've had this experience in my personal relationships. I have a tendency, as do many women, to want to accommodate men. If a man I'm relating to is unhappy with me, I feel very uncomfortable. I start feeling that I'm bad or wrong because of my point of view or behavior. I begin to give myself away to appease the man, do what he wants, and ignore my own needs.

Breaking my boundaries because of someone else's displeasure is ultimately self-defeating. I end up resenting him and myself. Nobody wins.

Many managers I work with are tested on their boundaries by their employees. There is always one that wants you to make a special case for her. She really needs extra time, money, or attention. If you break your rules for them, it usually blows up in your face. They quit, overly complain, or just become more demanding and less productive.

DIAGNOSTIC EXERCISE:

Write down ways you have allowed yourself to buy a ticket onto the Rescue Ride. Note what roles you have played in certain relationships, how your selection process ignored warning signals, and what you would do differently today if you could do it over.

_____

_____

_____

_____

_____

_____

_____

_____

_____

_____

_____

_____

_____

_____

_____

_____

_____

_____

_____

_____

CHAPTER TWELVE

~

SELF-NURTURING

*"People create the reality they need
in order to discover themselves."*
— **Ernest Becker**

As I've gone around the country teaching seminars on Deserve Level psychology, I have noticed that it's very easy for most of us to point a finger at ourselves or others and say, "That's how you messed up. No wonder your life isn't working."

The critical and negative voice sings so readily in our heads.

However you have been sabotaging yourself, it's what you needed to do to grow and learn. You didn't do it consciously to hurt yourself. It becomes the standard bearer to your new sense of self. It is the light that signals an end to the darkness, if you pay attention.

Sabotages are your unconscious mind telling you, "I'm not ready. I need more time, support or permission to achieve that goal I so desire."

Knowing that, it's important to embrace rather than abuse that message from your inner self. But how?

One of our hardest challenges to self-growth is learning to nurture and love ourselves. Most of us grew up putting ourselves down for every mistake and minor error. We learned it at home. Father may have criticized us because we did not clean up the kitchen or do that homework. Teachers, friends and siblings all had their part in pointing out our limitations. Now, as adults, we don't need them any more. We have learned our lessons well. We are our own best self-critics.

The development of a self-critical attitude is learned very early. Four-year-old Johnny is outside playing with his puppy. It is a lovely spring morning and they are having a fine time, jumping and chasing each other. Like most children, Johnny isn't very attentive to details. He leaves the gate open and the puppy runs out.

Crying, he goes to his mother. "My puppy dog ran away!" His mother has had a horrible day with problem after problem. This presents one more frustration than she can handle. She says angrily, "You bad boy! How many times have I told you to shut that gate?"

Now take the same situation with different characters. Four-year-old Steve comes running, crying, to tell his mother the puppy has run away. This mother says, "Oh, honey, you must feel awful to lose your puppy dog. Let's go see if we can't find him."

Johnny's mother criticized and added guilt to his pain. For him it was a lesson in self-rejection.

Steve, who was nurtured in his sadness and then helped to fix the problem, learned a positive alternative.

Both children feel sad at the loss of the puppy, but Johnny gets sadness plus guilt, which equals depression. Depression is not naturally healing. If Johnny learns to put himself down for every error, he can stay depressed and critical of himself all his life.

Steve also feels sad, but he has the support of his mother. Sadness plus nurturing equals grief, which is naturally healing. After a period of grieving, he will return to normal, his Deserve Level intact, and he will not be stamped with blame.

One incident won't make you feel self-critical, but hundreds of incidents do create deep personal doubts and low Deserve Level.

The emotional equation looks like this:

Feels	Receives	Emotional Reponse
Sad	Criticism and blame	Low Deserve Level and Depression
Sad	Nurturing	OK Deserve Level and Grief

Most of us have been raised on a steady diet of self-criticism rather than nurturing. We continue this tradition and treat the four-year-old in us in very critical ways.

CHANGING SELF-CRITICISM TO SELF-NURTURING

Dr. Eric Berne developed a model of human interaction known as Transactional Analysis (TA) to simplify psychoanalysis for public understanding. Berne taught that a person is made up of three ego states — Parent, Adult and Child. No matter what the age or life experience, each of us has a Parent, Adult and Child ego state.

The "Shoulds" and "Oughts" reside in the Parent ego state. "You should brush your teeth." "You ought to exercise." The Parent delivers all the instructions and "how-to's," along with judgments and opinions. The Parent has two different aspects, the Nurturing Parent and the Critical Parent.

The Adult ego state deals basically with facts. Not much emotion, just plain facts. "How old are you?" "What time is it?"

The Child ego state harbors our feelings. When we feel sadness, anger, joy or hurt, we are in our Child ego state.

Self-criticism occurs when there is an event, feeling or thought the Parent deems inappropriate and the Critical Parent comes on strong with negative messages: "You're so stupid. How many times do I have to tell you not to do that!" "You're selfish for wanting that. Stop it!" We all have our favorite negative fiction that we hear when we are self-critical. The Child in us feels shamed and blamed. The outcome blocks us in our movements, humiliates us for wanting something or embarrasses us for our feelings. We shut down emotionally and are at war inside ourselves. Usually the Child in us feels hurt, angry and sad.

One of the most frequent parent criticisms is that we are selfish or want too much. Who has not been told, "Your eyes are bigger than your stomach! You can't eat all that food!"

Some parents call their children selfish for their every want or desire. This criticism surfaces for big or little wants, from something as small as a dime-store toy to a car. The term selfish is used as a club to humiliate or evoke guilt. Alexander Lowen says in Bioenergetics, "When children are told that they are asking for too much, the parents are putting them down. A child never asks for too much, it asks for what it wants. 'Too much' is an adult evaluation that serves to make the child feel guilty for wanting."

This child grows up. This child is you or me — and when we want something, we immediately begin to feel guilty, selfish and undeserving. We curb our simplest wants out of fear of disapproval, our own or someone else's. We limit our Deserve Level.

Self-nurturing offers the alternative to chronic self-criticism. To get a feel for your own ability to criticize or nurture yourself, close your eyes and fantasize for a minute after you read these instructions. See the last incident of something you did that you didn't like. For example, you locked yourself out of the house, forgot to enter a check, lost something of value. Now listen to what you said to yourself. Have a dialogue between the Critical Parent part of yourself and the Child part.

Do you call yourself names, berate yourself, put yourself down? How is the four-year-old self feeling? Somewhat angry and depressed? Ashamed or hopeless? This is the dialogue that happens when you haven't lived up to your own expectations. You haven't been perfect.

Now try a different approach. Think of the same incident and see yourself as a four-year-old. Pretty cute kid, huh? This little person didn't mean to mess up. He/she is just learning or a little careless. Certainly excusable behavior. Be the child and share your feelings with the Nurturing Parent. "I feel stupid (sad, hurt, angry) that I _____." Elaborate on how you feel about the situation. Then let your Nurturing Parent come in and say, "I hear you. I understand that you feel _____. I'm with you and I'll support you. I love you." Continue this conversation for as long as possible. Nurturing means unconditional support for your being and your personhood. Because it affirms that you are lovable, it raises your self-esteem.

After you have finished this exercise, compare your bodily feelings between self-criticism and self-nurturing. There should be a great difference in your feelings of stress and tension between the two dialogues.

Let me give you a step-by-step account of learning self-nurturing. This dialogue came from a session with Barbara, a very successful therapist who has helped thousands of people overcome their emotional problems. In her own life she struggles with a phobia about making speeches. This is a dialogue she had between her Critical Parent, Inner Child and Nurturing Parent. See if it sounds familiar.

<u>Critical Parent</u>: "You can't do any speeches. You don't know anything. They will all laugh at you. Who do you think you are?"

<u>Child</u> (crying): "I know you're right. I can't do it. I don't have anything to say. I'm scared I'll mess it up."

(Makes an intentional switch to the Nurturing Parent.)

<u>Nurturing Parent</u> (soothingly): "I hear you. I understand you're scared. I believe in you. I'll help you through this."

<u>Child</u> (angrily): "I don't believe you. You've never helped me before. Why should you be there now?"

<u>Nurturing Parent</u>: "I understand that you're angry, and you have a right to be. You're right. I haven't been very supportive. I intend to change and stop criticizing you and start supporting you."

Child: "I don't know — you sound good, but can I trust you?

Nurturing Parent: "Just watch my behavior and give me a chance. I believe you can give speeches. You're bright and have lots of good information for people."

Child: "I feel better. I sure like it when you don't verbally beat me up."

Nurturing Parent: "I don't want to any longer. I love you and want the best for you."

Child (heavy sigh): "Thanks."

Faries McDaniel, M.S.S.W., developed this model for Interpsychic Nurturing. It applies to self-nurturing and nurturing of others, and can be used at any time.

THE SELF-NURTURING PROCESS

1)   To begin, state in the first person how you are feeling, from the Child ego state: "I'm hurting." "I'm worthless." "I'm stupid." Explore and encourage verbal owning of feelings.

2)   After this has gone on for a while, ask yourself what the Nurturing Parent in you would like to say to the Hurt Child. It might be something like, "I like you just the way you are." "You're okay." "I'm here for you, I'll take care of you." "I understand how you feel, and we're going to make it through this."

3)   Continue a dialogue between the Hurt Child and the Nurturing Parent. When you can feel (or hear, or see in changed body position) that the Child is feeling better, then to the Adult ego state.

4)   With the Child's feelings soothed, the Adult assesses the situation, looks at the facts, considers alternatives, and makes a decision.

5)   The Adult says in the first person, "I will do ..." "I have decided to ..." Now check out how you feel. You should be more relaxed and ready to make a good decision.

This self-nurturing exercise offers an excellent way to practice building up your self-esteem. Every night before you go to sleep, grab a pillow and hold it close to you. Pretend this is you as a four-year-old child. Let yourself tell you the feelings you are having: I'm scared or anxious, or whatever. Then see and feel your own Nurturing Parent come in and love that Inner Child. This exercise has soothed many a painful night for me.

Nurturing is a learned art. Most of us grew up feeling heavily criticized by well-intentioned grown-ups, and we became extremely self- and other-critical. To turn these negative patterns around takes tenacity and a devotion to the practice of not beating ourselves up!

Believing that I'm not such a bad person has helped me to keep myself committed to my own self-nurturing. I would never find the level of imperfections in others as awful as I do my own. Finally I decided to give myself a break and nurture my mess-ups and mistakes rather than be self-abusive. Guess what? I feel so much better about myself, and consequently don't create as many problems as I used to.

Right before completing my master's thesis I had an occasion to use my newly-developed self-nurturing skills. As I started to go in to give my oral presentation, panic hit me. What if I couldn't remember anything? What if I failed? Two years of hard work gone down the drain! I was working up a good anxiety attack when I remembered the nurturing techniques. I went into the bathroom, sat on the toilet, and talked softly to that scared little kid in my stomach. "I love you, it's okay. You'll make it through this. They won't kill you." Strange as it may sound, it really helped. I walked out relieved — and then saw my major professor standing at the sink. She smiled and said to me, "You're right, we won't kill you." Amazingly, I passed anyway.

This story of my master's thesis anxiety points out a significant fact:

The curse of high achievers is perfectionism. The curse of perfectionism is ignoring the 95% that is right and focusing on the 5% that is not.

We have a tendency to see the flaws, what's not done or finished in our business or personal life.

If you pay attention to the kinds of messages even the most well-intentioned families send, it becomes clear where we learned to accentuate the negative.

When the ratio is more like 20/80 — when everything seems to be going wrong — it is even harder for us to show compassion and friendship to ourselves.

The blunt truth is this: if we treated others the way we often treat ourselves, we wouldn't have any friends.

Fortunately for our friends, we usually know how to be supportive to them. The challenge is learning to do the same for ourselves.

It is easy to cheer for ourselves when things are going well. The challenge of self-nurturing is to learn to be loving to ourselves when things are not going well, when we are not perfect.

Dr. Wayne Dyer tells about a painting hanging in his living room which is so horrible that visitors comment, or painfully avoid commenting about it. Inscribed in the lower left-hand corner are the words: "To Dr. Dyer, I give you not-my-best." One client, who loved to paint, had stopped after being told she had no talent. At Dyer's urging to participate in activities she enjoyed, regardless of others' evaluation of her performance, she spent a thoroughly pleasurable weekend painting, and gave the results to him. Moral: We don't always have to be perfect or do our best. There's nothing wrong with taking an average bicycle ride or going for a mediocre walk. Always having to do the best can lead to paralysis and frustration — fearing to do anything because it might be less than perfect.

One of the best rules for managing ourselves and others is paradoxical:

Love them when they're down and challenge them to grow when they're up.

This is the opposite of what we usually do to ourselves. When our success is down and things are not going well, the temptation is to beat yourself up, tell yourself you are not any good.

That approach is not only unkind, it does not work. It simply drives the cycle down further. When the going gets tough is when it is most important to nurture yourself.

Nurturing is not about making excuses, rationalizing, blaming others. It is about comforting and respecting yourself.

If you can be loving, appreciative, and concerned about yourself and others, you can lift your energy. When you are doing well is when you can challenge yourself to do even better. That is when you have the energy to keep creating. When you are down, you don't.

Remember that we are not talking about accepting an unwanted situation. Self-nurturing does not mean accepting a 40% drop in sales with equanimity — it means accepting yourself even when those sales are down.

If you keep telling yourself, "I've got to be better, I'm not doing it right, I'm not making things happen," you predict and project from negative energy.

Self-acceptance means acknowledging your own efforts and energy, what you have done to try to make the desired outcome happen.

The difference is in our own self-dialogue. The difference is between a nurturing or a critical comment, a loving or an abusive action.

One of my most instructive lessons in self-nurturing came when I made an error. I was asked to appear on a local TV show to discuss a seminar I was conducting. It was 1979, and the other guest on the program was Barbara Bush. She was beginning the tour around the country promoting George for his 1980 presidential bid. I dimly knew who George Bush was but was confused about her relationship to him.

She and I chatted for a minute or two, and then I said, "It's so nice of you to go around the country promoting your son for the presidency."

There was a heavy silence, and then she replied, "I'm his wife, not his mother." I gasped at what I'd said, hastily made an excuse that I had to go to the bathroom. I sat down in one of the small meditation booths and tried to put my life back together, because I knew I'd just made the dumbest remark of my life. So I nurtured myself and reminded myself that my intent had been positive. My information was wrong, but my heart had been in the right place.

EXPERIENTIAL EXERCISE:

You can experience the difference between nurturance and criticalness with an exercise in imagination.

Close your eyes and pretend that your mind is a radio, and you can choose your station. Actually visualize a radio on the table in front of you.

Turn the dial to the station you usually listen to. Maybe it is full of self-criticism, or the kind of pseudo-acceptance that sounds supportive but really has a zinger in it. "Not bad, but you ought to be doing a whole lot better." Listen carefully to that same old static that is so familiar.

Now reach out and turn the dial to a new, positive station. Literally see your hand on the dial, feel it turn, until you tune in a new station. This one has only positive, nurturing things to say about you — not about the situation, but about you. "I'm with you. I believe in you. You are a good person. You can get through this." Listen for a while to these nurturing, positive statements.

Now turn the dial back to the old critical station, and feel in your body how you feel when you hear it again.

Once again, turn back to the positive station. Breathe deeply. Feel how you feel as you listen to that.

That experience happens in your own unconscious all the time, particularly when you are going into situations that require change, that require you to do something different — like grow and develop.

We all resist and have trouble with change. We may want it, but we have trouble with it. One of the important issues as you set about increasing your

Deserve Level is to notice that resistance, that fear. When you start to move toward getting more of what you want, be self-nurturing instead of self-critical. Nobody ascends like a rocket — we all take a couple of steps forward, then a step back. To keep your energy going in a positive direction, you have to develop the ability to be self-nurturing.

This is not an easy process to master, when you have been trained to believe that you achieve by harassing and criticizing yourself.

Another way you can keep yourself stuck in negatives is by not forgiving yourself or others — releasing the blame and regret over your actions or feelings. Feeling guilty or angry about someone or some experience bonds you to them in a negative cohesion. It's time to let go of these unresolved feelings.

FORGIVENESS EXERCISE:

> *Forgiveness is giving up all hopes*
> *for a better past.*
>   —**unknown**

Sit quietly with your eyes closed. Breathe very deeply. Now see yourself going down a flight of stairs. There are 30 steps. Slowly count them down, one at a time, until you reach the bottom.

At the bottom you enter a lovely room that is filled with a wonderful white light. Take a seat and see yourself talking with the person that you haven't let go of. Say everything you want to say about your hurt, frustration, or rejected feelings.

After you've said all you need to say, tell the person, "I forgive and release you. I forgive and release myself." See the two of you enveloped in the white light, and leave in peace.

Creating a nurturing environment within yourself can be greatly enhanced by having a support system that reinforces your needs. The next chapter tells you how to implement that experience in your life.

CHAPTER THIRTEEN
~
SELF-SUPPORT: WEAVING YOUR SUSTAINING NETWORK

"I want to love you without judging, join you without invading, invite you without demanding, leave you without guilt, criticize you without blaming, and help you without insulting. If I can have the same from you then we can truly meet and enrich each other."

— **Virginia Satir**

"What is real?" asked the Rabbit.

"Real isn't how you are made," said the Skin Horse. "It's a thing that happens to you. When a child loves you for a long, long time, not just to play with, but really loves you, then you become Real."

"Does it hurt?" asked the Rabbit.

"Sometimes," said the Skin Horse, for he was always truthful. "When you are Real you don't mind being hurt."

"Does it happen all at once, like being wound up," he asked, "or bit by bit?"

"It doesn't happen all at once," said the Skin Horse. "You become. It takes a long time. That's why it doesn't often happen to people who break easily, or have sharp edges, or who have to be carefully kept.

Generally by the time you are Real, most of your hair has been loved off, and your eyes drop out and you get loose in the joints and very shabby. But these things don't matter at all, because once you are Real you can't be ugly, except to those people who don't understand."

This lovely quote from <u>The Velveteen Rabbit</u> sums up our need for love and support. To "up" our Deserve Level and get what we want in life, we need the love and support of other people. Too often we don't allow this need for support to be expressed.

We live in a world where the pioneer mentality reigns. We are trained to be rugged individuals who take care of ourselves, are self-reliant and completely self-sustaining. Many times I've had people in therapy who have said, "I really don't want to be here. I thought I could handle this myself." These folks believe that seeking help, support or education is admitting weakness and failure. Their belief system contains the thought that they ought to be able to handle everything without assistance.

The reality of the world we live in is very different. We have moved to greater and greater diversification in all areas of life. That means the era of total self-sufficiency is over, and we need each other to create an integrated life. This mutual interdependence is the basis for our technology, culture and psychology. We need support from each other for our very existence.

What do I mean when I say support?

You are here because someone has loved you.

As children we ran to our parents when we needed psychological support. Our mothers primarily were the grounding forces when we felt emotionally overwhelmed. When hurt, angry, sad, we ran to them for support and reassurance.

If we were lucky enough to have "good enough" nurturing, we felt loved and lovable. We had an emotional foundation under us that we could depend on. If this support was consistent, we learned to rely on this source of nurturance, to count on its being there.

That let us be free to go out on our own, knowing there would be a safe harbor to return to if we should need it.

The challenge is to create support systems for yourself, to draw from your friends and mentors, to have others besides your spouse or sweetheart. Being another person's sole emotional support is too big a burden to put on a relationship.

"To give is to receive. That's the law of Love. Under this law, when we give our love away to others we gain, and what we give we simultaneously receive. This law is based on abundance."

This quotation from Gerald Jampolsky's best seller, <u>Love Is Letting Go of Fear</u>, expresses the wonderful duality of support and personal giving. If we give support or love, we then receive it back. Jampolsky says,

"The law of the world is based on a belief in scarcity. That means that whenever we give something to someone we lose it. We must then constantly be on the lookout to get our needs met. We must search and search to fill our empty well. We live in a belief of emptiness and constant need. We try to fill those needs through getting other people to love us or give to us.

"When we expect others to satisfy our desires we are constantly disappointed. They never do it right!

"When we are feeling depressed and finding someone to give us love is not really the solution, what is necessary is to give love to someone else. That love is then simultaneously given to ourselves. The other person doesn't have to change or give us anything.

"The world's distorted concept is that you have to get other people's love before you can feel love within. The law of love is different from the world's law. The law of love is that you are love, and that as you give love to others you teach yourself what you are.

"It's not charity on my part to offer forgiveness and love to others. Rather it's the only way I can accept love for myself."

Every one of us will hit nights of black despair. There will be dark times in our lives. It's then that you need your friends.

It isn't easy to feel vulnerable. When you feel vulnerable you may do a great deal of scurrying around to cover the feelings. That is when you need a friend you can call who believes in you.

Far from being a sign of weakness, the truth is that asking and receiving support from others is part of being a strong and self-sufficient person. Really strong people value themselves and don't like feeling hurt or depressed. They take care of their human needs. They ask for support and aren't critical of themselves when they need it.

As you are building your support system, it is important to have friends who are living in the ways that you want to live. The friends we associate with invite us to their level of experiencing life. If your friends are all fast-track professionals who are proving themselves in their corporate worlds — and you want to get off that train, have a baby, and enjoy life's softer side — they will subtly or even directly tell you to live by their rules. You may find yourself "out of sync" with them and feeling lonely.

That is a clue that you need the addition of others who share your current life view. It is difficult for all of us to be empathetic or supportive of someone whose lifestyle is radically different from ours. That's why we need affiliations with friends in our particular life phase. Such friends can affirm what we're doing and what we believe in, and can encourage us to become what we want to be.

We must all be "goosed" to greatness. None of us will go there without some resistance. That's what a good support system does for you. It believes in you so completely that you are moved to action.

One of our struggles can be in assessing who in our system is helping us move forward and who is holding us back. Old friends from college can go in different directions, develop different values as the years go by. They may still care, but your life paths are different now, have simply grown apart. No one is wrong, you are just no longer right for each other.

The same experience can happen in marriages and families. If your support system has become critical or negative about what you want in your life, ask them to be more respectful and supportive. If you allow the people closest to you to undermine your values, you will get depressed, frustrated, defeated. Ultimately, we educate other people about how we expect to be treated.

Doesn't it make sense to gravitate toward people with whom you have mutual respect, who are doing what you want to be doing, people you admire and believe in? They will make it easier for you. That is the whole premise of mentoring or networking — to have people help you along the path.

When I was a beginning speaker I went to the National Speakers Association meeting, where I met a famous speaker, Joe Charbonneau. He was giving a presentation that captivated the audience with his humor, wisdom and his own personal power. I sat there and thought, "Gee, I wish I could be as good as he is." After the presentation I gathered my courage and approached him. I said, "I'm just beginning my career and would appreciate any help. Would you listen to this demonstration tape of one of my seminars and give me some feedback?"

He smiled and said, "I'd be glad to." He opened his briefcase and put in the tape, and I saw that he had about a hundred others in there as well. I thought, "Well, that's that. He'll never have time to listen to my tape."

Five days later he called me from Cleveland, Ohio, and said, "Sit down, I have five pages of notes on how you can become a great speaker!"

I felt like crying. I didn't expect such a supportive, helpful response.

Joe taught me something very important that day. I had debated whether to ask for his help and expertise. I didn't want to bother him or intrude. All those reasons for sabotaging my needs went through my mind, when the truth was, if he didn't want to help me he wouldn't have done anything. By asking I was giving him a gift to enjoy himself through being supportive.

As he said, "One of the best aspects of my career is to watch and encourage new talent. I remember when I was just starting, and I want to pass on all the encouragement I received."

A motivational speaker tells the story about being on his return flight from giving a speech. The man sitting next to him, when learning what he did for a living, said, "Aaah, that motivational stuff doesn't last. You get yourself all pumped up for a while and then it wears off."

A passing flight attendant overheard him and said, "Well, a bath doesn't last either, but it's still a good idea."

If you think about it, food doesn't last either. Exercise doesn't last. Everything in life needs to be renewed and nurtured. We feel hungry, we eat, we feel full and in due time we get hungry again. Life is change.

The same thing is true about motivation. It is important that we keep motivating ourselves and others, because we all run out of it.

Motivation is the dynamic tension between the push of discomfort and the pull of hope.

You have to have some discomfort to be motivated. You have to want something, to yearn for some desired goal. There has to be some discomfort about where you are before you are motivated to change your life. You have to want to lose ten pounds, make more money, or live more serenely.

At the same time you have to have some hope. You have to believe it is possible to change, that what you want is attainable. You have to know it's possible by experience. You know someone who <u>has</u> lost ten pounds or made more money or become serene.

You need to have discomfort and hope in balance, with approximately equal amounts of each, to be motivated.

We aren't always feeling balanced or motivated. Sometimes we have <u>too much discomfort and too little hope</u>. What happens when the scales tip in that direction? We're grumpy, unhappy with how our life is going. This becomes the usual gripe session. "Nothing's right, the economy stinks, my love life is a mess."

What we need at that time is hope. We need to be loved through our despair and discomfort. If we go to a friend and explain our problems he says, "Yeah, the world's a mess, no one can do well in this economy, just forget women, it never works out anyway," he has given us more discomfort and pushed us farther into the motivational slump.

We can get out of balance on the other side as well. We can have <u>too much hope and too little discomfort</u>. I know this sounds like "Margaritas on the beach," but it doesn't work out that way. Too much hope looks more like inertia, being in a rut, not feeling challenged about your career or love life. It's all very predictable and routine. You'll hear it when someone is talking about himself and making statements like, "I've been in insurance sales for twenty years. I know what to do. I'm doing okay, it's steady income."

What's missing is the excitement, the juice, the passion. It's all gotten routine and deadly dull. So, what's needed? Some discomfort to realign the motivational balance.

None of us get out of our ruts gracefully or easily. We need to be challenged to do something to bring back our feelings of life and passion.

Mid-life crisis is just such a shaking up. Whatever you're doing in mid-life, you want to do the opposite. If you're married, you want to be single; if you're single, you want to be married. If you have kids, you want to be rid of them; if you don't, you want them. It's a great time for reflection and reassessment of what is really important to you.

The formula is very simple. Whatever side you have the most of, you need more of the other side in order to get remotivated. Too much discomfort: get hope. Too much hope: get discomfort.

As a friend or manager, understanding this motivational equation can give you the answer of what to do when someone comes to you in a crisis. Love them when they're down (low hope), goose them to greatness when they're up (high hope)!

THE STROKE ECONOMY

Another important component of our support needs is a positive stroke system. The expression "strokes" comes from Transactional Analysis. By definition, strokes are any form of positive or negative attention, given as a form of acknowledgment.

To the extent that we get positive strokes in our lives, we feel energized. To the extent that we get negative strokes, we feel diminished. A lot of the environments we live in are comprised mostly of negative strokes. The rule is, "We only pay attention to people when they do something wrong."

The way to motivate people to keep achieving well is to acknowledge what is good, what is already working for them. This is true of children, mates, employees, bosses.

If you haven't had time to read some of the management best sellers in the last five years, let me sum them up for you. Ken Blanchard, The One Minute Manager, said to find someone doing something approximately right and positively acknowledge him for it. Tom Peters, In Search of Excellence, said the companies that are doing the best are the ones that invest in their people. All of the information points to the same outcome: people want positive acknowledgment and will work hard to get it.

What you pay attention to is what you get more of. What you choose to focus on is what will grow. This is the most basic tenet of behavior modification.

Most of us have had the experience of having a small child bring us their drawings for our inspection. What we do is look at the drawings and say something like, "This is a beautiful drawing. I'm going to put it on the refrigerator so everyone will see it!" Within ten minutes we are presented with twenty other drawings! All of us want positive strokes.

A stroke economy is based on these things:
1)   Giving strokes.
2)   Receiving strokes.
3)   Asking for strokes.
4)   Saying NO to strokes you don't want.

Giving strokes: If you are committing to a positive stroke economy, go home to your family and tell them what is good about them. The most nurturing kind of stroke is about who they ARE, not just what they DO. This is where a child's self-esteem is formed, being told he is a neat kid, irrespective of whether he has just pleased you by performing some task. In our society it is easy to hug and appreciate small children, but somehow we stop doing it as they get older. That's too bad, because teenagers, grown-ups, elderly parents all need positive strokes acutely.

Receiving strokes means allowing positive strokes to come in. A lot of people are trained to deflect appreciation ("Oh, no, it wasn't that good a meal, I didn't put enough salt in the gravy.") It is easy to discount the positive — not to hear it, not to allow it in. Even in the midst of abundance, you can starve to death if you will not allow yourself to be nourished. Right now, give yourself permission to allow yourself the kind of pleasure that comes from letting positive strokes in.

Asking for the strokes you need is <u>simple</u> enough, though for some people it is not so <u>easy</u>. If you have had a tiring day — or a great day — call up a friend on Friday night and say, "Let's go out to dinner, let's go out and talk. I've missed you." Ask for attention and strokes, and gather people in your life who will give them to you.

Say no to strokes you don't want. If someone is giving you mixed messages, or telling you something negative that you think is inappropriate, be willing to preserve your own integrity by saying, "I don't want that. I don't want to be treated that way." It may be scary the first few times, but that is how you can protect your stroke economy and keep yourself fueled with fairness and positive energy. This is not to discount someone's genuine complaint, only to preserve your right to be respected.

THE EMOTIONAL BANK ACCOUNT

Steven Covey talks about an "emotional bank account" that everyone establishes with everyone else. This bank account uses emotional acknowledgments as the currency, not money. Deposits are measured in friendly morning hello's, calling someone on the phone, hugs, sending flowers or remembering birthdays. Anything that shows someone you care.

Obviously, we all want to have high emotional bank balances with people we care about. The higher the deposit side, the more we'll have to draw on when we need to make a withdrawal.

SAME-SEX SUPPORT

In our life struggles we need support not only from our intimate partners but also from friends of the same sex. This same-sex support is crucial in promoting and protecting our intimate relationships.

Jim Miller, M.A., and Eleanor Greenlee, M.A., in their presentation at the Northwest Bioenergetic Conference explained this need.

"As we grow up we need to separate from the parent of the opposite sex. This usually happens in adolescence. At age twelve or thirteen, when a boy tries to separate from his mother, he'll turn to his father for support.

"If his father isn't available for that support, then the boy is left with mother. The boy is then faced with an identification problem. He needs his father to be supportive of his identity as an emerging young man. If his father isn't there he's in trouble, because his mother is the only person he's getting support from and he needs to separate from her. That's almost impossible to accomplish. We all need support too badly to separate from the main person who is giving us our support.

"This boy then has a problem of identity. He needs a father to show him how to be a man. His father isn't there for him so he learns his emotional attitudes from his mother. (The same is true of girls, just switch the gender.)

"The problem with this shows up most obviously in later life in intimate relationships. If a boy doesn't have father's back-up and support he can't fully separate from mother. He then attempts to separate from the women in his life by developing equivocating and corrective behavior."

You'll see these behaviors in couples all the time. The wife says, "That's a lovely blue sofa." The husband responds, "It's really not a true blue, it's got gray in it." He corrects her and subtly tells her she isn't accurate. The problem with this exacting behavior is when it's chronic. When a man needs to separate from his mother he becomes evaluative and corrective of the current woman in his life. This behavior drives her crazy. She can't do anything right or please him. This pattern is prevalent in both sexes when there is incomplete separation from the parent of the opposite sex.

What needs to happen is to be able to openly disagree and say "no" to your partner. The problem is you can't do that if you don't feel support for your identity from the same sex. You'll be too afraid of losing the support you have from your intimate partner. You can become slick, devious and hostile, but you don't admit your hostility. Something happens and instead of just being mad, you deny the anger (out of fear) and become very unreasonable.

If this scenario sounds too familiar, you need more resources for personal support than your intimate partner. You need good loving friends of the same sex. As Jim Miller said, "I realized that a great deal of the battling and conflict I had with my first wife had little to do with her, but was my attempt to finish my separation from my mother. When I realized this, I called her and apologized for some of my reactions. I have learned when I'm in a battle with a woman to go to my male friends for support."

The need for same-sex support is fundamental in maintaining intimate relationships with the opposite sex. You can't get from your partner the acknowledgment or separateness or identity that you need. You can't always get your separate opinion supported because sometimes it's in opposition to your partner's opinion. Your partner can't support your identity, at least in heterosexual relationships, because he/she doesn't know what it feels like to be a woman or a man.

The only solution is to turn to a friend of the same sex and build a support system.

SUPPORT AND SUCCESS:
JESSE'S STORY

Jesse was a fifth-grader living in Missouri. Jesse's year began with his father being taken to prison for writing a number of invalid checks to try to feed his family. Jesse was left at home with his mother and three sisters. His job was to come home after school and take care of his sisters — fix their dinner, help them get their homework done, and get them bathed and put to bed. His mother worked three jobs just to put food on the table and keep a roof over their heads.

Jesse was very responsible. He took care of those little sisters without complaining, but it was a hard time for him. He didn't feel good about himself. He missed his father, he only got to see his mom for about fifteen minutes between her jobs, and frankly, he was depressed.

He didn't have any friends, because when the other kids were playing, Jesse was home taking care of the smaller kids. At age ten he was, in essence, a single parent.

Jesse went to school every day and sat on the back row and looked down at the floor. He didn't interact with the other kids — he didn't know what to say, so he gave up trying.

But he had a teacher who believed in him and supported his growth. Every day as she was working with the kids, Mrs. Skogan would put her hand on his shoulder and say, "Jesse, how're you doing? What can I do for you today?" And he knew that she loved him. She was the only person that whole year who touched him, and that touch made all the difference.

Jesse knew that Mrs. Skogan held a high value on education, and he would have done anything for her approval. He got out of fifth grade, then sixth grade, and finally all the way through high school — which was amazing, because he had a lot of pressure from home to leave school and go make money.

Jesse even went through two years of college. He started a manufacturing firm and did phenomenally well.

Twenty-five years later, Jesse went back to that classroom and he sat in his old chair again. He watched Mrs. Skogan do what she did so well, which was to love those kids and believe in them.

At the end of the class, he said to her, "You probably don't remember me, but I'm Jesse, and you saved my life. Your love and your support changed what I would have done with myself. I came back to thank you."

With that, he handed her an envelope. Inside it was a check for $50,000. He said, "I want you to know that all the love, all the caring, all the support always comes back."

So it is with all of us. If you will allow yourself to believe that you deserve the best, that belief will help achieve it — not only for you, but for everyone you come in contact with. By helping each other reach a higher level of deserving, we can change the world, one person at a time.

CHAPTER FOURTEEN

~

I GOT IT! DESERVE LEVEL SUCCESS STORIES

"Whatever you can do, or dream you can,
begin it.
Boldness has genius, power and magic in it.
Begin it now."
Goethe

All of us want the best for ourselves. In the words of T.S. Eliot, "between the thought and the action falls the shadow." The shadow of our dreams is self-sabotage. The overcoming of our self-sabotage is the challenge of adult development. Most of the time, we do not simply ascend to glory and goal attainment. We struggle. We take two steps forward and one back. The hardy and courageous among us persevere to finally reach our dreams. Those are happy days!

I'd like to share with you a few of the hundreds of letters and calls I've received that are cause for celebration. These real folks have attended my seminars, or read the book and used the tapes, and have taken the information to heart. I invite you to celebrate with them and to say to yourself: "THIS COULD BE ME!"

As the German Philosopher Goethe so eloquently stated:

Until one is committed there is hesitancy, the chance to draw back, always ineffectiveness. Concerning all acts of initiative and creation there is one elementary truth, the ignorance of which kills countless ideas and splendid plans: that the moment one definitely commits oneself, then Providence moves too.

All sorts of things occur that would never otherwise have occurred. A whole stream of events issues from the decision, raising in one's favor all manner of unforeseen incidents and meetings and material assistance which no one could have dreamt would have come [one's] way.

CAREER CELEBRATIONS

Getting out of your own way in the workplace can lead to extraordinary breakthroughs and success. Here are the stories of a few people who found permission to let go of limiting beliefs so they could achieve their goals. Their common theme is being able to get permission from the past to move into a brighter future.

I never realized until I attended Pat Pearson's workshop just how much we all sabotage ourselves!!!

Five years ago, I decided to quit my full-time job as a Chemical Engineer to pursue my own business. I have so many dreams and goals! As an Independent Sales Manager with Weekenders, the success of my business is highly dependent on the success of women I train and sponsor into my unit.

Looking back, I can identify distinct times during the last five years when I have "brushed up" against my deserve level. Prior to Pat's training, I never realized we had such a thing! Now I use Daily Affirmations to keep myself on track, and I use the principles that Pat teaches to help my Fashion Coordinators "up" their deserve levels. When I use Pat's techniques, we have extraordinary results. When I don't, our results are mediocre.

I've read a lot, listened to a lot of tape programs, and tried lots of techniques. What I love the most about Pat's training is that she not only describes what is "going on" in your head, but she gives you simple, practical techniques that we can all learn in order to make the changes needed to "get out of our own way" and achieve our goals and dreams. In March of 1997, I reached the highest position in Weekenders — that of National Sales Director. Thanks for all your help!

Susie Nelson
Orlando, FL

It is not often that you attend sales training or a seminar and have a significant, life-changing experience. That is the kind of effect Pat's training has had on my life.

A few years ago, I attended Pat's training at KLOL radio. At the time I was an average performer — kind of stuck in a rut. That year I billed about $500,000, and was in the middle of the pack.

Pat helped me redefine my life with a new vision. I came from a family of five, in which no one has been a big success — so my own level of performance was about all I thought I could expect. Certainly, as Pat teaches, this is far from the truth. By increasing my "Deserve Level" I was able to increase my sales to over $1 million, and the following year, I led the entire pack of sales reps!

Since then, I have continued to challenge my goals and dreams, processing events positively, instead of in my old negative way. Asking "why not more" instead of "why does this happen to me?".

After KLOL, I was promoted to Sales Manager at another radio station, then moved on to an even more successful position as a Financial Consultant with Merrill Lynch. My income has increased from approximately $40,000 a year to $140,000 a year, and it continues to grow.

A big thanks goes to you, Pat — keep up the great work, because we both deserve it all!

Nestor Vicknair
Merrill Lynch
Houston, TX

Deep down inside, I always felt that I deserved the best...but I didn't always know what kept me from getting it. Since attending Deserve Level seminars, and practicing the techniques, I know I deserve the best that my dreams have to offer, and how to go about getting them to come true!

Pat's work with my radio sales staff brought amazing results with their approach to business. Doubts went right out the window. We experienced only fresh, new and positive attitudes about goal achievement and taking responsibility to make it happen! With what we learned from Deserve Level training, each year we outperformed the previous year by ten to thirty percent.

Now, I'm starting a new career and my own business and utilizing my Deserve Level techniques. I've upped my "Deserve Levels" and gotten out of my own way!
Muriel Funches
Dallas, TX

When I first heard Pat Pearson speak, I encountered my limitations and success-blocking fears. At that time I was living in my office, sleeping in the closet. Pat's tapes turbo-charged my focus and my ability to go for the dream. I'm out of the closet now and regularly making $7,000 in a morning! Pat really made the difference.
Peter McGugan
Best-Selling Author, Speaker, and Broadcaster
Austin, TX

I attended Pat's breakout session at the Century 21 International Convention, and enjoyed it very much. I am a Marketing Consultant, Franchise Sales, with the Century 21 Regional Office in Dallas. My territory includes thirty-four counties in East Texas, and twenty-eight parishes in northern Louisiana and southern Arkansas.
I practiced Self-Talk as Pat taught, and it has worked! I achieved goal number one, and am well on my way to achieving number two. For the first goal, my wife and I are going on a free Cruise in October with nineteen other Marketing Consultants from across the United States who qualified also. I intend to continue Self-Talk from now on.
Carroll E. Bobo, Marketing Consultant
Century 21 South Central States, Inc.
Irving, TX

John Maguire, the general sales manager of WRKO Red Sox Radio in Boston, uses affirmations as a management tool with his sales force. His account executives write performance goals (dollar amounts) and number of prospects to contact per week. When they reach these goals they are rewarded with bonuses and prizes.

To help them focus, he has them state their goals in the form of sentence-completion affirmations. Here are the affirmations of Bill Ebben, one of Red Sox Radio's top producers:

I am billing one million dollars for Atlantic Radio and Red Sox Radio.

I am making $90,000. I am going to make $120,000.

I am living in a brand new house. We will be living in a home of our own. Why? Because we are not renewing our lease — we have affirmed it.

As is true with all the account executives, Bill has signed (with John) a Commitment Agreement which reads:

I hereby commit that I will give my best possible effort to achieve my goals. I am accountable to deliver daily the enthusiasm, the activity and the performance necessary to reach my goals in a timely professional manner. I am accountable to myself to do what it takes to be RED SOX radio's top biller!

Bill Ebben is billing $850,000 after six months in radio. At this rate, he will earn $95,000 in his first full year. The year before he earned $23,000. Extraordinary success by any standard!

One of my dear friends was struggling with trying to get pregnant a second time. Amid all the pressure of precise timing, taking of temperatures, and rushing to procreate, the joy of the experience was being lost. As she said, "This is really hard work!" I suggested that she do an affirmation that reinforced the joy of creating a beloved child. Three weeks later, while running between appointments, I picked up a telephone message that said her name and the message "The affirmation worked!" A lovely and gifted daughter named Jane is the result.

All the people in these stories had attended my seminar and heard me ask them to let me know when they reached their goals. I told them that if they'd let me know, I would take them with me when I reached <u>my</u> goal, which is to be on Oprah Winfrey's show talking about this book!

AT LONG LAST, LOVE
Self-sabotage, because it is unconscious, happens to everyone — even the people who teach how to prevent it! My story is similar to those of many who have struggled with deserving it all (in all life's important areas, not just one).

Pat's Story: Finding Love on a Tour Bus?
I was speaking internationally and traveling ten times a month to exciting places. My income was soaring, but my spirit was depressed. I had gotten divorced several years earlier and was lamenting my single, lonely state. I sat in lovely hotel rooms, watching late-night television, eating Oreos and feeling very negative about myself and men. My Self-Talk was awful. I'd say "There are no good men left. They're all dead or married." I knew I was sabotaging myself.

164

It was then, out of my own pressing need, that I'd become entirely focused on Deserve Level Dynamics. I changed my negative Self-Talk to Positive, and gave myself New Permission to believe there was at least one well-matched, lovable man for me in this big world.

My affirmation was: "I am married to an attractive, loving, secure man who deeply enjoys life." I also made a list of forty qualities that I truly wanted to have in a husband, such as: he has his own friends; he has high self-esteem and self-confidence; he has a strong faith; he does silly, fun things and is spontaneous. These attributes spoke to how he lived and felt about himself. And then it happened!

On a trip to Alaska, in a tour bus, I met my future husband. I was speaking at a Mary Kay Cosmetics event in Anchorage, and as a side pleasure trip, I took my stepdaughter Heather to Daneli Park. We were riding in a park tour bus when we heard an adorable tow-headed boy tell anyone who would listen that his Dad's clothes smelled bad! He was announcing that they were so dirty that they could stand up in the corner by themselves. We immediately began to giggle. As soon as he had found an audience, eight-year-old Timmy gave us the full story.

Timmy and his father, Steve, had been traveling on the train and lost their luggage. Several days had been spent in the same jeans and shirts. As we laughed about the perils of travel, I noticed that behind the Dallas Cowboys cap and sunglasses there was a very attractive man.

After a day of panning for gold and horseback riding, we all decided to have dinner together. Tim had told me his Dad raced cars as a hobby. I gave Steve the keys to my rental car for after-dinner sightseeing. We were ardently looking for moose when he backed the car into a tree! We laughed about his only going forward on the track.

The next day, after saying goodbye and exchanging business cards, I was driving with Heather back to Anchorage. I was smiling to myself and she said "You really liked him, didn't you?" I said "Yes, but he's geographically undesirable. He lives in California, and I live in Dallas. It's impossible to date long distance."

Ironically, twenty-four hours later, in the airport rental-car garage, Steve and Timmy appeared out of nowhere and were walking in front of us. I rolled down my window, and we greeted each other like long-lost friends. At that moment, I felt a tap on my shoulder, and a heard a voice saying "This man is too important to miss. Pay attention!"

A year later we were married in a seaside ceremony, and I'm the happiest I've ever been.

Wanted: Sensuous Jewish Woman

You helped me make my dreams and wishes come true. I had always believed in positive affirmations, but never used them consistently. After reading your book, I decided to use my affirmations on a daily basis, instead of listening to the same radio music during my commute to work. I took my list of affirmations which included: "I am dating a highly-attractive, successful, compassionate and sensuous single Jewish woman." I repeated this, plus other affirmations regarding business, finances and health.

I am so happy to let you know that I met the woman of my dreams last February, and we got married this past May. My wife Chari is truly what I was looking for in a partner for life. It has also shown me that you do not have to settle for second-best if your goals are realistic. Chari keeps telling me that she is so surprised that I was still single and not taken. And she loves traveling as much as I do.

I have also achieved some of my other affirmations, such as the yearly sales of my company, and I am approaching my salary goal. As I attain my goals, I reevaluate those goals and my affirmations. I truly believe that your ideas on attaining goals are right on the mark! Thanks for helping make my dreams come true!
Jay M. Bernten
Chestnut Hill, MA

How to Marry the Boss
I had a list of what I was looking for in a mate, and it was not like I was exactly scheming to marry a millionaire. I just wanted someone who was bright, successful, with a strong character, who valued most of the things I do. Randy and I knew each other from work, and were good friends. I already had a pretty good idea that he fit the bill. The only problem was convincing myself that it was okay to go after this guy (after all, he was my boss), and convincing him that I was the person he was looking for.

Randy actually sent me to Pat's workshop on Deserve Level, thinking it would help me. Little did he know that sending me to that workshop would be the catalyst for changing both our lives. Understanding Deserve Level reinforced things I already knew, but the timing was perfect to give me that extra push to go after my goal. Now we're both glad Randy sent me!
Mary and Randy Pennington
Pennington Performance Group
Dallas, TX

THE WEIGHT OF THE WORLD
One of the greatest challenges many of us face is in the area of body image. In today's world where

"thin is in," and "thinner is inner," almost every woman and many men feel like complete failures if they aren't perfect "10s." And most of us aren't. Here are some stories that show that no matter what's happening in the rest of your life, self-sabotage can still be present.

Oprah's Ups and Downs

A *People* magazine article that charted Oprah's diet dilemmas told the story of Oprah's moment of truth at the Emmy Awards.

The 5'7" talk show host, 42, whose weight had fluctuated as much as the Dow Jones industrial average — and had been covered by the media almost as passionately — reached a lifetime high in June 1992 of 237 pounds... Oprah Winfrey sat in the audience at the 1992 Daytime TV Emmy Awards desperately hoping she wouldn't win. "I was in the front row trying to keep my too-fat knees together in a ladylike position," she writes in the introduction to Make the Connection: Ten Steps to a Better Body—and a Better Life... "I was thinking, 'God, let Phil win. So I won't have to waddle my way up the stage with the nation watching my huge behind.' I was 237 pounds — the fattest I'd ever been."

Following is an excerpt from the book...
...Oprah Winfrey!"

I was stunned. Stedman and my staff were cheering. I wanted to cry..I was the fattest woman in the room.

The next day I met Bob [Greene]. That's when my life began to change. Up until that point I had spent a lifetime dieting and depriving myself, then overeating and gaining even more weight. It all started when I arrived in Baltimore at the age of 22 in 1976...I lived in Columbia, Maryland, across the street from the great Columbia Mall. They had some of the best food stalls known to womankind...On weekends I'd go from stall to stall. Sometimes I'd order something from every booth. I didn't realize at the time that by overeating I was trying to fill something deeper. The fact that I was lonely, somewhat depressed, and having a hard time adjusting to the new job never entered my mind.

By that fall I had gained 10 pounds...By the end of the year I was 150 pounds.

When I moved to Chicago in December 1983 to host AM Chicago, the local morning show...I thought this could be a new chance to get motivated and finally get the weight off...Three or four times a week, we'd hit Rush Street, a great Chicago strip lined with restaurants...A month later, I was shocked to find I weighed 180 pounds. One day while doing a show with yet another diet expert...I told the story about the time I'd been trying another diet back in Baltimore.

I had been doing very well, then I made the mistake of visiting my old haunts — the food stalls at the mall. But I didn't succumb. Instead, I literally ran out of there. After getting home, I was overwhelmed by a compulsion to eat...Food was my drug.

The show started on the first day of January 1984. The next four years, I would move from 202 to 218...Then I heard of Optifast, a fasting and diet supplement program. I saw this as the road to freedom...

I was 211 when I started on Optifast in July 1988. By the fall I was 142 and into a pair of size 10 jeans....What I didn't know was that my metabolism was shot...There was nothing my body could have done but gain weight.

It was time to stop the supplement and return to real food. I was 142 for one day. The next day I was 145. In two weeks, I was 155. I felt hopeless.

Outwardly, I was becoming more popular and successful. Inside, the burden of weight was always there. I tried not to be depressed about it...I decided to try again. I booked three weeks at a new spa in Colorado.

When Oprah met Bob Greene at the Doral Telluride Resort and Spa in 1992, she writes, "I thought, He must think, 'What a wallapalooza. I'm supposed to work with her?'" Greene, however, saw a courageous woman. "...I had tremendous respect for her, as I do for anyone attempting the challenge of permanent weight loss."

Until then, Oprah worried about what she ate; Greene encouraged her to exercise more regularly and, equally important, to think about why she ate. Winfrey says Greene helped her realize that, for her, food...was the solace she turned to whenever she felt anxious or insecure.

"For me, food was comfort, pleasure, love, a friend, everything," she says. Now "I consciously work every day at not letting food be a substitute for my emotions."

[Oprah] has adopted a steady diet of self-awareness — and this latest attempt at getting in shape seems well past the fad stage. Since starting with Greene, Oprah has run marathons, maintained a healthy weight and, she says, "If you're angry, be angry and deal with it," says Oprah. "Don't go eat a bag of Ruffles."

"Nobody can hurt me any more than I hurt myself," says the trimmed-down Oprah. That's a classic definition of self-sabotage. Wonderfully, Oprah has now changed her sabotage to success!

A Great Weight Lifted

I have struggled with my weight for some time and after much agonizing over what to do and which direction to take, I listened to Pat Pearson's "You Deserve the Best" tapes on affirmations. These tapes have made all the *difference in my ability to lose weight and, more importantly, <u>maintain the weight loss</u>. I believe the difference has to do with the tapes helping me focus and get clear <u>consistently</u> with my goal to lose weight.*

My affirmation is: "Nothing tastes as good as thin looks," and I use that affirmation over and over. The tapes helped me see how important it is to be constant and vigilant about my affirmations — I have lost ten pounds so far and now want to <u>keep it off</u>!

What a blessing! Thank you, Pat!

Susan Ellis
Dallas, TX
P.S. Susan has lost over 40 pounds and looks gorgeous!

OWNING HER LIFE

After reading (Pat's) book three times in a year it finally began to sink in. With my final reading, I actually did the exercises, and boy, what a difference! I remember what you said about how we only retain about 20 percent of everything we read, so I made my own crib notes from the book and put them on audio tape along with my affirmations.

I religiously listened to that tape for 21 days straight and memorized some of the techniques and quotes. This began to make a profound difference in my life. I began to realize how unhappy I was, even though to outsiders my life looked great. But I was the one who had to face it each day. I discovered that not only was I unhappy, but my actions were counter-productive to the life I wanted to lead.

Through this work I found out what I really wanted to be doing, and how I could achieve it. I started to take some time out to discover me, and the possibilities unfolded.

Within two months... I moved to New York City. I am living in a tiny studio in the East Village and I am so happy! I get so filled up with a sense of joy, it sometimes brings tears to my eyes. I used to be drowning in boredom...it is exciting to find out what its like to live your OWN life.

I am closer to my family now than ever before, and not just geographically. (Pat's) work helped me find one of the best resources for unconditional love and support I have been missing for so long. ...the happiness I found was only possible because her book opened my eyes to the immense joy I could find in life. ...and I am living proof that by insightful questioning of one's goals and dreams anyone can gain the confidence to find infinite joy in their own life.

Debra L. Johanson
New York, New York

COMPANIES: FROM SABOTAGE
TO SUCCESS

Many companies have been created by people who have experienced some personal setback or sabotage of their dreams. I have had the pleasure of working with both of the companies profiled here, and in the process I discovered that what galvanizes each one is the dedication and commitment of its leadership.

Passion for People: Mary Kay Cosmetics

During the Depression, young Mary Kay Ash started off selling brushes and household cleaners through Stanley

Home Products. She then joined another company as head of its sales training. After eleven years, she came to work one day to discover that the male assistant she'd been training for almost a year had just been made <u>her</u> boss, at twice her salary.

When she protested this injustice to her superiors, she was ignored. The business policy was hidden but clear: if you were female, you were supposed to be part of the support team, not management. Mary Kay quit her job.

That's when her passion was born. She made a decision which later became a credo: she would create a sales business in which women would be treated respectfully and their self-esteem fostered. Unlike traditional organizations with quotas and caps on income, there would be no ceiling on the amount a representative could make.

She invested her life savings of $5,000 to start her new company. A month later her husband collapsed at the breakfast table and died of a heart attack. With children to support and a fledgling business, she plowed ahead.

In stark contrast to the attitudes of the company she had quit, Mary Kay made the Golden Rule her major mission statement. A sincerely religious woman, she has consistently urged to members of the Mary Kay enterprise that they put God and their families before their careers.

Because of her vision, thousands of women have become moderately to wildly successful in the Mary Kay business. There are thousands of beauty consultants and sales directors driving complimentary automobiles and at least 100 women who have earned commissions of a million dollars or more.

To visit a Mary Kay convention is to be in the midst of passion. Of course there is the usual conviviality and enthusiasm expected at such a sales convention, but there is also a mentoring atmosphere among women devoted to supporting each other to deserve the best.

Their excitement is understandable. Women with no business experience, as well as restless professionals, have found an entrepreneurial opportunity in which they'll not only be able to make excellent incomes, they will be appreciated along the way. One woman says, "Mary Kay calls you her daughter and looks you dead in the eye. She makes you feel you can do anything. She's sincerely concerned about your welfare."

Mary Kay's big heart has not only enriched her consultants, it has paid off for her as well. The Ash family fortune is estimated at $320 million — from an initial investment of $5,000. Mary Kay is currently the best-selling cosmetic line in America. The Company was born to honor the individual spirit of women who want to make a difference. And what a difference they have made for themselves and others — both financially and personally.

As Mary Kay wrote to me in a personal letter:

Dear Pat:

How thoughtful of you to send me a copy of your book. Obviously we are both in the business of helping people develop their talents and abilities to the fullest. My heart was warmed to hear your assessment of our Mary Kay sales force. I'm sure you can appreciate that I am very proud of the calibre of women who represent our Company.

God bless you for helping people change their lives for the better.

Sincerely, Mary Kay Ash

This woman has touched the lives of hundreds of thousands of women, and by her example, led them to get out of their own way and deserve the best.

The New Vision "Rocket Ship"

This incredible success story is of a family's resurrection from devastating personal and financial tragedy to resounding success.

The year was 1994, and the Boreyko family comprised the top distributors for a network marketing company. Between the parents and children, there were six Boreykos actively working in that company. At the highest point that meant $350,000 a month coming in. And during that same year, tragedy struck. The Boreyko family discovered their beloved mother Dottie had cancer. She died within ninety days of the diagnosis. Just before Christmas, the family suffered a devastating financial blow as well. The company the Boreykos had worked so hard to make successful declared bankruptcy. Losses of such magnitude can sabotage people for years, but as B.K. and Jason like to say, "God has a hand on this company."

Brothers B.K. and Jason Boreyko wrote the first plan for New Vision on a cocktail napkin on a Southwest Airlines flight, and started the company March 20, 1995. They dedicated their "New Vision" to their late mother, and her memory is richly honored. Along with their sisters, Karen and Lynne, and their Dad, Ben, they share partnership in the company.

Not only is this company founded on their mother's spirit, it is a tribute to their father as well. As B.K. told Success Magazine: "He brought 4,000 people from our other company to New Vision. They'd worked with him for twenty years. He always said 'If you're not having fun, you're not doing it right!'" Well, these guys are doing it right!

New Vision is a network marketing business that focuses on selling nutritional supplements such as essential minerals and vitamins. All this is accomplished through high technology and good old personal relationships. They keep it simple for their distributors. They have state-of-the-art ordering abilities, along with non-confrontational sales tapes for the products. This allows distributors to give people tapes, which reduces the anxiety often experienced when trying to sell someone. They can field questions and take orders from the comfort of their homes. There are no required night meetings, no hype, just thousands of happily-involved distributors.

Success Magazine called New Vision a "Rocket Ship" of the network marketing world. So how did this idea become a rocket ship? Dream big dreams!! In the Success article, B.K. stated, *"Jason said 'Let's set a goal of $8 million per month and 100,000 distributors by March 30, 1997.' That's $100 million per year, I said, 'Man, are you crazy?' We did it 11 months ahead of schedule. We just had a convention of 2200 people in Vegas, and he stands up on the stage and says, 'We're going to do $1 billion by [the year] 2000 with one million members.'"*

Soon, we will all be reading books about the Boreykos. They have united the scintillating components of personal integrity, excellent products, high technology and caring about their people to truly create a New Vision.

Finding The Connection

Mary Williams represents the fabulous Noevir line of cosmetic products. Finding herself "stuck" in reaching her personal and professional goals, she had to look closely at how her own limited thinking concerning success was standing not only in her pathway to reaching sales goals, but was limiting the people who looked to her for inspiration and support. Working in a one-on-one relationship with me, she encountered a new way of thinking, and learned to get out of her own way. Let's hear from Mary...

Because of Pat's keen insight into the nature of network marketing and all the related problems, I invited her to meet in a group setting with all my leaders. She brought to them a new confidence and new deserve level concerning their business. But to their delight, she zeroed in on each individual's unique struggle, and offered some specific resolutions for them.

Focusing on the critical "deserve level" and belief systems that created that level for each individual freed us up to deal with some demanding personal issues, while at the same time addressing some self-confidence and self-esteem issues in our business group.

Having an understanding of how to identify and affect those permissions from the past that color my beliefs today has changed the way I work, and more importantly, allowed me to help each person in my downline identify those same limiting beliefs that kept them from growing. I know voices from the past will always be there, but now I know how to quiet those voices and add one of my own that says, "You can do it, Mary!"

CHALLENGES AS YOU GO TO THE TOP

Sabotages can even occur within a highly-successful career. Here are two stories of bright, energetic people who overcame the challenges of mid-career sabotage.

Ann Sherman has been a very successful Mary Kay Director for a long time. Every year the company could count on Ann and her unit to create $500,000 in revenues. Successful but stuck, Ann truly didn't believe she could generate any more business than she had been thus far. Her negative beliefs kept her on a high but not fulfilling level of achievement. But Ann wanted to increase her revenues and go on the fabulous trip with the other top directors, while helping many women be successful in their Mary Kay businesses. So she was frustrated and stuck in a mid-career sabotage.

At a company conference, the Promotions Manager who was passing in the hall said, "What's wrong? Are you psychologically stuck on half a million? Don't you know this company needs people like you to be in top management?"

That did it! Ann got mad — not at the company, or at herself, which is self-defeating — but at the reality of being stuck. She took personal responsibility for her sabotage and said, "This is going to change!" She harnessed her anger and focused it to revamp her business.

We worked together to create new positive beliefs about her business such as, "I'm making more money and having fun, while hosting five guests at every skin-care class." Her motto became STRIVE FOR FIVE.

By using affirmations and refocused passion Ann has made a 25% increase in her business in the last six months. She is creating $750,000 this year, and she's only beginning her rise to fame.

"Prosperity is the most difficult thing in the world to handle." — Dave Rudman, $200 Million Texas Wildcatter

Peter Thomas, the charismatic, wildly successful entrepreneur behind Century 21 of Canada knows the challenges of maintaining high success levels. At a business conference in Hawaii he heard from a friend about the concept of Century 21 franchising real estate brokerage. As Peter says in his book <u>Never Fight with a Pig</u>,

...I felt a rush of adrenaline go through me as I grasped the concept...It combined two old ideas: real estate and franchising. Soon I was brushing off the sand, placing a phone call to Art Bartlett and leaving the conference for Los Angeles on the first plane I could catch that day.

Peter Thomas was able to purchase the exclusive rights for Century 21 Real Estate of Canada. He doesn't discount the part luck played, but he says forcefully, "It was not luck that put me on that plane to California to clinch the deal for the Canadian territory; that's called seizing the opportunity. The lucky part was that the timing was perfect."

Within the next few years, there were Century 21 offices from coast to coast in Canada, and Peter Thomas was a millionaire. As Century 21 prospered, the ever-energetic Peter got into other business deals. One deal was guaranteeing real estate for a developer. This venture almost sabotaged his phenomenal success. He inadvertently got caught in a huge real estate downturn and ended up owing $30 million against his guaranties.

Peter really needed his positive vision and goal focused attitudes in that troubled time. By using the principles in this book, particularly goal-setting, negotiation and visualizations, he came out of a potential disaster with his company intact.

Subsequently Peter sold Century 21 for many millions of dollars, and is now using his energy in other real estate businesses. As he said in a personal letter to me after one of my seminars:

"All of us do have our own 'Deserve' levels. Although mine are about as high as anyone's I know, after your seminar I wrote down some new goals. Did I tell you that after that seminar I walked out and bought myself a new Rolls Royce Corniche convertible — because, as you indicated, I deserve it!"

FINDING SUCCESS WITHIN

Over the years I've had the pleasure of working with hundreds of Mary Kay Cosmetics directors. Here are a few of their success stories...

Sandy Miller *was in the final stretch for National Sales Director qualification when I started working with her. A warm, enthusiastic person, she simultaneously took on two tough challenges: losing 25 pounds at the same time she was working overtime to achieve the highest level of leadership in Mary Kay. Daily affirmations and a strongly focused belief that anything was possible if you want it enough resulted in a beautiful, slim Sandy ascending the* stage to celebrate her career victory. Now, a year later, Sandy is still doing fabulously in her career — and maintaining her new slim look!

Barbara Coffey is a dedicated and talented Mary Kay director who was challenged by a mid-career recruiting sabotage. She had been a great recruiter, effortlessly sharing the gift of May Kay with many people to steadily build her unit. She even had two of her directors spin off. Within a space of only two or three months, both of these directors quit the business. These personal and professional losses wounded Barbara and created a great deal of grief. When I started working with her this backlog of unresolved grief, and the fear that if she put enormous energy into new recruits — extending herself professionally and personally — it might happen again, was sabotaging her joy in recruiting. She just didn't have the same spark she had before.

What she did have was "spunk," and a strong determination to be better. She took on her two issues — resolving the grief and anger, and refocusing on her recruiting. She was challenged by Suzanne Brothers, who offered a trip to Bali and Singapore to the Director in her unit who recruited the most people in a certain time period. Barbara loves being with Suzanne and really wanted to be the one who won that trip. Through visualization and affirmations she experienced the fun and excitement of shopping and strolling around Bali. Strengthened by that picture, she created a very focused affirmation, "I am easily and confidently recruiting three personal, qualified business associates each month." Yes, you guessed it. She won! Barbara is Bali-bound.

Alia Head *is a beautiful, bright young woman who chose Mary Kay Cosmetics over a legal career. In 1991 her organization had five Directors. Deciding that she wanted to grow not just a successful organization, but an extraordinarily successful one, she used a variety of techniques for growth, including "Deserve Level" training and thinking. Pat Pearson's individual consultations with many of her directors helped them overcome personal challenges, and build successful businesses of their own. Her own personal faith in God has been an important factor in her life and her success. Her organization has grown from five in 1991, to 35 Directors in 1998, and she has several Directors-in-Qualification whom she will support as they reach their goals for the new millenium.*

Amber Bostock's challenge came after moving to Dallas from Raleigh, North Carolina, and having two small children. The energy formerly focused on her business was drained away by the demands of settling into a new city and caring for two very young children without any support system. Feeling frustrated by her inability to perform as she had before, Amber noticed that her Self-Talk was getting more and more self-critical, draining her flagging energy even more, But Amber was a fighter and a winner, so she took on this challenge and turned the negative dialogues around to Positive Self-Talk. Instead of saying, "Why should she want to talk to me?" she changed her dialogue to, "I am easily and confidently sharing the vision of Mary Kay with sharp women who will get it!"

Slowly, over months of effort she came back. Amber's turnaround culminated with her being selected "Most Improved" in her area, and winning a special trip for her excellent efforts.

There are challenges at each step and potential sabotages that will have to be resolved. That's the process of life. You can resolve any sabotages you encounter. That's the message of this book and all the lives and stories that are contained in it. As Eleanor Roosevelt said,

The future belongs to those who believe in the beauty of their dreams.

What does deserving the best amount to if we're not happier because of increasing our deserve level? That's a question I've asked myself. The answer, I believe, is in this quote from Abraham Lincoln:

Most people are about as happy as they make up their minds to be.

Happiness and quality of life is largely a matter of choice and attitude. Wealth, knowledge, health and love all help to move us in the right direction. But many inspirational stories remind us that ultimately the human spirit is the final determiner of happiness.

People magazine told the phenomenal story of Oseola McCarty.

"During the seventy years that Oseola McCarty washed clothes for well-to-do families in Hattiesburg, Miss. the frugal washerwoman never took much time for herself. But after the outpouring of affection and acclaim in 1995 when she donated a large part of her life's savings — more than $150,000 — to the University of Southern Mississippi, the diminutive 88-year-old decided, perhaps for the first time in her life, to go for the glamour.

"It has been a breathless 18 months for Oseola McCarty, who had ventured out of Mississippi only once before news of her generosity brought reporters from as far away as Argentina to the door of her small wood-frame house in the summer of 1995. Since then she has traveled to more than a dozen cities to collect civic awards. Harvard University presented her with an honorary degree, Roberta

Flack serenaded her at a National Urban League gala, and on Dec. 31, McCarty pulled the switch that lowers the New Year's Eve ball in Times Square. Winning a 1995 presidential medal was another highlight of McCarty's hectic year.

"For McCarty, who never married and has lived alone since 1967, the biggest return of her gift to USM is a new joy in life. `She's kind of come out of that shell she was in,` says friend Ledrester Hayes, whose granddaughter Stephanie Bullock, 19, is one of two African-American students to have received an Oseola McCarty endowment Scholarship to USM.

"Now that friends are likely to drop by, McCarty has perked up the living room of her house on Miller Street, where for years she was kept company by a dog called Dog and a pig called Hog. Even in retirement, McCarty can't really relax. Last summer, Shannon Maggio, an editor from Atlanta's Longstreet Press, came to McCarty's front porch to help her write her first book, <u>Simple Wisdom for Rich Living</u>, which has sold more than 35,000 copies since it was published last November. This wonderful woman shows all of us that Deserving the Best is an inner attitude and choice."

Finally, as Hugh Downs reported on *20/20*, when that TV show interviewed a group of centenarians they found some very interesting results. They found that all of these people, who had lived over 100 years, shared four traits.

1.   *They had a positive mental attitude.*
2.   *They were able to handle grief and loss.*

3.   They had a purpose and spiritual dimension in their lives.
4.   They had a passion and focus on something to do and create.

By getting out of their own way and deserving the best from life, they are shining models to us all.

As George Burns said at age 98...

> *"I've fallen in love with my future."*

May you do the same.

~~~

NOTES

"LIVE AND IN PERSON"
PAT PEARSON, M.S.S.W.

With over 20 years of experience as both a clinical psychotherapist and motivational speaker, Pat Pearson is an exciting presenter with a passion for inspiring audiences to claim their own personal excellence.

Pearson travels throughout the country and the world sharing ideas on professional development, sales success, leadership and employee productivity with some of the world's leading companies, including: IBM, Mary Kay Cosmetics, American Airlines, Travelers Insurance, Century 21, Southwestern Bell Telephone. She is a top-rated speaker for professional and trade groups such as Meeting Professionals International, among others.

Her powerful keynote speeches and seminars are informative as well as entertaining. Unlike mere "motivational" speakers, she provides concrete, proven, practical methods for mobilizing an individual's resources. She blends the experience and expertise gained from her 20-year practice of psychotherapy with in-depth understanding of the methods, motivations, issues and blocks that affect the sales success of network marketers and other sales and marketing professionals.

Pearson, who practices daily the advice for living that she presents in her seminars, resides on the Southern California Coast with husband, Steve Frohling.

For Seminar or Product Information Contact:
1-800-374-4574 or 949-718-0311

Pat Pearson c/o
Pearson Presentations
37 Monterey Pine Drive
Newport Coast, CA 92657